The Ethics of Inquiry in Social Science

The Ethics of Inquiry in Social Science

Three Lectures

J. A. BARNES

DELHI
OXFORD UNIVERSITY PRESS
BOMBAY CALCUTTA MADRAS
1977

Oxford University Press
OXFORD LONDON GLASGOW NEW YORK
TORONTO MELBOURNE WELLINGTON CAPE TOWN
IDADAN NAIROBI DAR ES SALAAM LUSAKA ADDIS ABABA
KUALA LUMPUR SINGAPORE JAKARTA HONG KONG TOKYO
DELHI BOMBAY CALCUTTA MADRAS KARACHI

Printed in India at Universal Advertisers (Printing Division),
E-2, Jhandewalan Extention, New Delhi-110055
and published by R. Dayal, Oxford University Press,
2/11 Ansari Road, Daryaganj New Delhi–110002.

Acknowledgements

I am much indebted to the Institute for Social and Economic Change, Bangalore, and to its Director, Dr V.K.R.V. Rao, for the invitation to spend a couple of months at the Institute as a Visiting Fellow. I am particularly grateful to Professor M.N. Srinivas for first giving me the idea that I should visit south India, and to him and Mrs Rukmini Srinivas for all they did to make my wife and me welcome in Bangalore. I much enjoyed meeting other members of the Institute and greatly appreciated their hospitality and intellectual stimulation.

I am also very grateful for the professional and domestic hospitality extended to us by the Indian Institute of Management, Bangalore, and in particular by Professor M.N.V. Nair. My wife and I were especially pleased to be able to spend so much time discussing everything under the sun with those members of the Institute with whom we shared accommodation.

I hope that these lectures may serve as an expression of my thanks. Frances Barnes made very helpful comments on an earlier draft. The lectures are printed here more or less as I gave them at the Institute for Social and Economic Change in August 1975, with only minor corrections.

Churchill College
Cambridge,
19 October 1976

J. A. B.

Contents

1
Social Inquiry and Pluralist Society

The Distinctive Features of Social Science

Although the origins of social science can be traced with reasonable plausibility back to classical antiquity, it is only in the twentieth century that recognition has been granted by the general public to the existence of a specific corpus of accumulated knowledge, cultivated and added to by a specialist group of professional social scientists. Ancient founding fathers lend an air of respectability to any pedigree, however dubious their claims to paternity may be, and it is, therefore, not surprising that some historians of social science have tried to claim for their discipline descent from Plato and Confucius, from the Mahabharata and the code of Hammurabi, and from numerous other classical writings (Becker & Barnes, 1961). Yet despite these efforts to demonstrate that the social sciences belong to the same tradition of learning as other established academic disciplines, with the implication that they share the same general characteristics, there are nevertheless many present-day scholars, particularly in the more conservative universities, who still refuse to accept the academic credentials of the social sciences. These critics argue that if the label 'social science' refers to anything definite at all, it cannot be the name of any proper academic field of study but only of some hybrid mixture of meaningless jargon and pretentious platitudes and truisms.

As a professional social scientist I regard this description of social science as inaccurate and incomplete, even though I am aware of the type of evidence on which this false view is based. Nevertheless these critics provide an appropriate point of departure for these lectures when they say that the social sciences differ radically from what they perceive as proper academic disciplines, divided into the natural sciences and the humanities. Against them I argue not that the social sciences are like, or should become more like, the natura sciences and/or the humanities but rather that our perception of what academic disciplines should be must be enlarged so as to include the social sciences, with their distinctive and often academically unsettling characteristics.

One of these distinctive qualities, one of the ways in which the social sciences differ fundamentally from both the natural sciences and the humanities, lies in the relations between the academic practitioner, in this case the social scientist and, on the one hand, the phenomena he (or she) studies and, on the other, the wider society that feeds and clothes him while he carries on his work and which, maybe, listens to him when he reports on what he has found out. These relations, particularly the relation between the social scientist and the people he studies, are quite different from the corresponding relations found in the other major branches of learning. It is for this reason that many problems and questions arise in the social sciences that either take another form or do not occur at all in the humanities and the natural sciences. In particular, it is because social science is essentially an activity in which human beings study themselves that complex ethical questions have to be faced as an abiding concomitant of that activity. In these lectures I discuss some of these questions and try to show how they arise and why they cannot be avoided. I hope that in at least some instances I manage to indicate how they may be answered satisfactorily, but I realize that I leave many questions unresolved.

In ordinary speech we sometimes refer to the natural sciences as hard science and to the social sciences as soft. If we have in mind the kinds of data used by the two branches of science there is some justification for this popular usage. But if we think in terms not of data but of problems, these epithets must be interchanged. The intellectual task of the natural scientist is greatly simplified because his data are, comparatively speaking, hard and reliable, and because the separation between him and the natural phenomena he studies is clear-cut. The social scientist, however, deals with data that usually are unreliable and fuzzy and, more importantly, his relation to the phenomena he studies is two-sided. The people he studies not only talk, they also talk back to him. Consequently it is his kind of science, rather than that followed by the physicist or chemist, that should be called hard if we wish to indicate the difficulty of the task he faces. Certainly the small amount of scientific success achieved so far in social science, as compared with natural science, suggests that social science is indeed a hard undertaking. Ethical problems constitute a major component of its intrinsic difficulty.

In this first lecture I sketch a model of society and of social inquiry in which the main ccmponents are (1) social scientists engaged in empirical research, (2) citizens whose behaviour and attributes constitute the subject-matter of the inquiry, (3) gatekeepers who sometimes control access to these citizens and (4) sponsors who supply the resources so that research can be carried out. In the second lecture I use this model in discussing selected instances of situations in which the divergent and convergent are interests of these four parties have given rise to ethical questions. In the third and final lecture I discuss how this model has been realized in different ways during the historical development of social science. I distinguish tbree phases: first, the beginnings of organized social research; then the age of imperialism and buoyant industrialism; and finally the post-imperial age of the present day. In other words we begin with a theoretical model, go on to consider empirical evidence and end by identifying historical trends.

Ethics and the Various Disciplines

Ethical questions are not confined to the social sciences; they are raised in both the natural sciences and the humanities. But in a sense these questions are extrinsic and contingent in these two fields of learning whereas, so I argue, in social science ethical questions are intrinsic, ubiquitous and unavoidable.

Ethical questions certainly arise in the humanities. We need recall only that Socrates was condemned to death in Athens for the corruption of the young. But for the most part the study of the humanities raises issues relating to the internal structure of the body of practitioners, issues concerned with plagiarism and priority of publication and the like, rather than with the relations of the disciplines to the wider society. Likewise in the natural sciences there have been serious ethical questions, particularly in recent years when the destructive capability of natural science has grown so dramatically. I need mention only ethical questions connected with atomic bombs, germ warfare and environmental destruction, and more recently with genetic engineering. But these illustrations show that in one sense they are not intrinsic to the natural sciences. For the ethical problems that have arisen in connection with, for example, atomic bombs are not concerned with cruelty to atoms or to the various elementary particles with which nuclear physics deals, but with the effect that nuclear reactions may have on fellow human beings. Yet human beings, as such, do not enter into the theory of physics at all; they never appear as terms in physical equations, whereas they do appear in the propositions of social science. It is only when events and processes in the natural world come to have an impact on the world of human beings that ethical questions begin to arise for natural scientists (cf. Laszlo & Wilbur, 1970). Fellow human beings are the essential ingredients of the social scientist's stock-in-trade, the recurrent terms in his equations. Hence for him the ethical consequences of his professional activities are ever present and, even though they are not always salient and pressing, they can never be ignored.

I have spoken of fellow human beings. In this expression the basic difference between natural science and social science may be discerned. The natural scientist is, like the rest of us, at one level of analysis simply a large collection of atoms. But in no sense does he interact with the objects under his microscope or in his cyclotron as one collection of atoms interacting with another fellow set. The social scientist does however, both in his inquiries and in his analysis, interact with the people he studies, with citizens as I call them for purposes of exposition, precisely as one human being to other human beings. Social science is the study of human beings by human beings and in a significant sense the social scientist is no more, and no less, a citizen than the people he studies. What he does and what he discovers has significance for them as well as for him, even though this significance may not be identical for the two parties. In current jargon social science, and sociology in particular, is reflexive science (Gouldner, 1970 ; O'Neill, 1972).

With these considerations in mind we can understand why during the last fifteen or twenty years social scientists have given increasing attention to questions of professional ethics. Since the end of the Second World War, and particularly since the middle '50s, the amount of social inquiry of all kinds has increased enormously. During this period ethical and political questions, which previously had arisen only sporadically and which could be dealt with piecemeal, have had to be faced in a more systematic and institutionalized manner. Some professional organizations have issued ethical codes to which their members are expected to conform. Drafting these codes has typically generated a great deal of argument and controversy, as for example in connection with the codes proposed for the American and British sociological associations. Other professional organizations have debated the matter for years, only to come to the conclusion that no code is needed for them, or that individual members should each work to his or her personal code. The great increase in the amount of money available for social research since 1945 in many industrialized countries has at the same time led the bodies dispensing this money, the sponsors in our terms, either government agencies or private foundations or even the isolated patron or firm, to develop codes of practice which specify in some detail the ethical constraints that must be accepted by the scientists they support (cf. Portes, 1975).

More recently citizens, the people whose behaviour and attributes form the subject-matter of social research, have increasingly begun to question the part they are called upon to play as informants or respondents to questionnaires or as participants in laboratory experiments. Individually or collectively they have begun to ask 'What's in this for me? Why should I answer your questions? If you ask me, why shouldn't I ask you?' This reaction is not entirely new, for from the earliest beginnings of systematic social inquiry in the nineteenth century there have always been individuals who have refused to cooperate, who have given misleading answers to questions, remained silent, or have obstructed research in a variety of ways. However it is, I think, only within the last fifteen years or so that uncooperative citizens have begun to challenge significantly the course of research in principle, as distinct from merely obstructing it in practice. The best known instances of this objection in principle are provided by those Blacks in the United States who refuse to give information to interviewers on the ground that the interviewers are White or else that, though Black, they are stooges working for Whites. Similar responses have been made by Australian Aboriginals and North American Indians, and this type of refusal in principle to cooperate seems to fit with some of the statements of supporters of the Women's Movement.

These recent refusals differ importantly from those earlier instances where, for instance, tribal peoples refused to reveal their religious secrets to probing anthropologists. In these cases the rationale for refusal was usually that the anthropologist was not an initiated member of the tribe and that, therefore, he lacked the qualifications essential for access to the secrets, or that, even if he had acquired the necessary qualifications, he would pass on the secrets to the unqualified world at large through his publications. Thus for instance Australian Aboriginals have sometimes allowed male anthropologists to view and photograph sacred rock paintings but have been outraged when they have found these same paintings featured on the dust covers of books available to Aboriginal women in public libraries. In cases such as these there was no objection to, and perhaps no awareness of, the process of social inquiry as such but only to inquiries being made about particular matters that should properly be hidden. The new objections now being made are not dependent on the content of the questions, which may indeed relate to such open and public topics as names and ages and place of residence. The objections are to how the inquiry is carried out, the role assigned to the respondent in that process, and the use to which the information will be put. In the extreme case there is simply a blanket objection to social inquiry as such, particularly when the inquiry is being made by government or when respondents believe that their answers to questions will be filed in some computerized data bank, liable at any time to be retrieved and used to harm them. The sentiment is that individuals should be able to live their lives as they please and that they are under no obligation to reveal any information about themselves to anyone. Sentiments of this kind were heard quite widely in Britain at the time of the 1971 Census.

Some commentators on the conduct of social research have written about these reactions by citizens and sponsors as if these were unfortunate repercussions that should somehow be avoided as far as possible. Negative reactions by citizens, so these commentators argue, can be minimized by good techniques of field inquiry, while interference by sponsors can be combated by publicity or collective professional action, or by appeals to an image of disinterested scientific inquiry in which knowledge appears as a free but hidden commodity waiting only to be discovered so that all mankind can benefit thereby. They assert a norm of unrestricted freedom of scientific inquiry that should always prevail over conflicting norms.

I think this view is entirely mistaken. The resources for research are scarce; money does not grow on trees for even the purest of scientific objectives. Its use for research rather than for succouring the needy or pampering the rich has to be argued and justified, and it is the sponsor who provides the money who has to be convinced by the argument. In my view the question is not whether a sponsor should impose conditions but rather what these conditions ought to be. Likewise to assert that hindrances to data collection interposed by informants and respondents can be overcome by good investigative techniques alone is to treat citizens as if they are merely the objects of research, rather than fellow human beings with interests that should be respected as much as those of sponsors and of social scientists themselves. The question is not how refractory objects of research can be manipulated without trauma but rather how negotiations can be effectively concluded with other human beings so that the social scientist achieves his research aims without violating the aims and expectations of the citizens he studies.

Citizens and Gatekeepers

My use of the term 'citizen' is unusual but deliberate. The people studied by social scientists are usually referred to as the objects of research or the subjects of experiments. Neither term is satisfactory, for to call people objects is to equate them with things, with no rights and interests of their own. To call them subjects, as is standard practice in psychology, is not much better. In linguistics, subjects may control verbs but in real life subjects tend to be themselves controlled by rulers and governments rather than to be in control of their own situation. Furthermore the nouns 'subject' and 'object' are associated with the adjectives 'subjective' and 'objective' which have their own ill-fitting set of connotations. 'Researchee' (Record, 1967 : 37) sounds terrible. It seems preferable to avoid these labels and to refer to the people whose lives are being studied as citizens, thus stressing that they are, or ought to be, both autonomous, responsible individuals possessing rights and duties and, at the same time, members of some collectivity, a city or community.

In practice, citizens are not always their own masters; this is often the case with those groups of citizens which social scientists seek to study. In most countries any social scientist, as a citizen, has a right to ask another citizen for information, and it is within the discretion of the latter to decide whether or not he will provide the information requested. But suppose the citizen to whom the request is made is not just a man in the street or a householder in his own home. What happens when he is an employee working in a factory or a nun secluded in a convent or a tribesman living on some segregated reserve, or just an ordinary citizen living in a country different from that to which the social scientist belongs?

Before the investigator can begin to negotiate his request for information with the citizens who are to provide it he must first gain the permission of, or perhaps surreptitously bypass, other individuals or organizations who control access to them. These are the gatekeepers—managements who can give permission for a research worker to enter a factory, headmasters who can allow a social scientist to enter a school, departments of indigenous affairs who can provide permits to enter restricted areas, and so on. In some instances the sponsor of a research project may also be the gatekeeper but more often he is not. A social scientist may well find that gaining access to the people he wishes to study may be as difficult and lengthy a process as gaining financial support for his work. When citizens are separated from the social scientist in this way, negotiation between scientist and gatekeeper may be necessary before the main inquiry can begin. Gatekeepers sometimes maintain that their own interests are nothing more than the true interests of the citizens for whom they are responsible, who cannot themselves articulate what they need, but in practice the citizens are likely to perceive their own interests differently.

Thus in planning and carrying out his research the investigator has to deal with three distinct entities, the sponsor, the gatekeepers and the citizens. He has to offer somewhat different benefits to them in return for their cooperation and support. The situation is complicated because these are not monolithic entities; there may be a plurality of gatekeeprs, there is certain to be diversity of interest among the citizens, and even sponsorsmay be internally differentiated. No wonder social inquiry is hard science!

There are still two general questions to be discussed before we can consider the lessons to be learnt from specific instances in which ethical issues have been raised. First, what are the implications of the fact that social inquiry consists of one specialized group of citizens, social scientists, interacting with another set of citizens specialized in some other way? Second, what kind of society must there be before it makes sense to speak of the divergent interests of citizens, sponsors, social scientists, and gatekeepers? A good deal has been written in answer to the first question, and I shall concentrate my own comments on the phenomenon of feedback. The second question, which I think is more interesting, has attracted much less attention from writers on methods of social inquiry.

Let's take the first point first. Social science deals with the characteristics of fellow citizens rather than of inanimate nature, but the consequences of this difference vary greatly with the type of inquiry that is being made. At one extreme are social surveys where a sample of individuals, on one occasion only, are asked a set of questions about their attributes and opinions. The citizens who supply the information remain anonymous and any relations they may possibly have with one another are ignored; indeed, most sampling procedures are designed to ensure that as far as possible the individuals selected are independent of one another. Any previous participation in social surveys is ignored; for statistical purposes we assume that we are dealing with virgin respondents. Under these conditions there is little effective feedback between citizens and investigators though, at a later stage, when the results of the inquiry are published or put to use, the interests of the citizens may be affected.

At the other extreme is the kind of inquiry, say for example an investigation of the working of management-worker collaboration in a factory, in which a team of investigators remains in contact with an enduring group, in this case the workforce of a factory, over a period of several years. The team is likely to spend a long time negotiating with the citizens about how the study shall be conducted, its scope and duration, and eventually about how its findings shall be reported. During this process not only do significant relations develop between individual members of the team and individual citizens, but the citizens also to some extent transform their relations with one another. The inquiries may bring to the surface latent tensions and may force individuals to make explicit assumptions that previously had been only implicit. This may lead to changes in procedure in the factory, or to some shift in the balance of power between management and workers or between one sector and another. The book or report that follows the inquiry, however it may disguise the identity of the factory, will be recognized for what it really is by at least the citizens who have participated in the inquiry, and may well become an authoritative document that can be appealed to in future struggles and negotiations. Hence it is only fair that the citizens should be associated with the writing of the report, even if only to provide them with an opportunity to repudiate it.

Most inquiries fall between these two extremes. The encounter between investigator and citizen may be longer and more meaningful than in a sample opinion-poll but may not be as protracted and structured as in the factory example. For instance a community study, focusing on local politics, if it has any success at all, will bring to light and record in cold print actions and relations that previously may have been obscure or hidden or preserved only in the ambiguous medium of oral tradition. Yet, though the interests of the citizens are clearly affected by the publication of this material, there is unlikely to be an organized collective body, corresponding to the Works Council in our factory example, with whom the publication of the report can be negotiated. Indeed, with a study of local politics, it is likely that approval of a report by one faction will entail its repudiation by rival factions.

Traditional anthropological fieldwork provides another kind of intermediate example. The incoming ethnographer has to negotiate with the tribesmen even to secure a roof over his head and throughout his period in the field he has constantly to persuade citizens to devote time to talking to him and to tolerate his participation in their daily activities. But the community to which the citizens belong is likely to be different from the ethnographer's own political and intellectual community, so that it may be difficult to convey to them the objectives of his inquiry, or at least its theoretical implications. It may be quite impracticable for him to negotiate about what shall be published. In these circumstances the ethnographer incurs a heavy responsibility for protecting the interests of the citizens in their absence. This responsibility is particularly onerous because tribal peoples are so often in a powerless situation and are unable to protect their own interests effectively. Furthermore, tribal communities typically form part of political structures characterized by lack of consensus, so that actions that are meritorious or obligatory in tribal eyes may be regarded as illegal or unnecessary by the politically dominant group. Hence in reporting on illegal activities the ethnographer has to be particularly careful that the information cannot be used to the detriment of the citizens whose confidence he has enjoyed.

Deception

In the examples given so far I have indicated the need for negotiations as between fellow citizens, on a basis of formal equality, though in practice this cannot always be achieved. But in some types of social inquiry the notion of honest negotiation is difficult to apply even in principle. The difficulty is more fundamental than in the tribal example. It may be difficult in practice to explain to a tribesman that the reason why an ethnographer would like to know how he addresses his mother's mother's brother is, say, to test Festinger's theory of cognitive dissonance or Dell Hymes' notions of genealogical extension, but nonetheless a resourceful ethnographer can go at least some way towards conveying the general nature of his intellectual interest. But some other forms of social inquiry depend for their success on deliberate deception or concealment of aims. Citizens may be deceived in two ways; an inquiry may be carried out by disguised scientists, so that citizens do not know that it is being made, or else the inquiry is apparent but the scientist conducting it lies to the citizens.

In covert inquiry the scientist disguises himself as a citizen and interacts with others as if he were merely one like themselves. They do not know at the time, and indeed may never know, that he is studying them (Scott, 1965 : 261–74). This technique has been used where the scientist seeks information which he believes the citizens would wish to keep secret from an outsider but which they may be willing to impart to a newcomer who identifies himself with them. Several studies of rule-breaking in industry and commerce have been made in this way (e.g. Roy, 1952). Covert research has also been undertaken in situations where the scientist believes that the presence of a recognized observer would drastically alter the behaviour of the citizens, not because they wish to conceal illegal or deviant activities but because the observer would become a new focus for their attention. Thus for example a scientist posed as a patient in a mental hospital in order not to attract unwanted attention from the 'real' patients whose behaviour he wished to study (Caudill, *et al.*, 1952; Devos & Vogel, 1973 : 234–5).

Both kinds of covert inquiry are similar to spying yet we cannot therefore simply infer that they are unjustifiable. A discussion of the ethics of spying lies outside the scope of these lectures but it should be clear that even if spying is sometimes justified, a scientist cannot claim to be operating under the banners of science and espionage at the same time; he must choose one or the other. Yet even in terms of his commitment as a scientist to the pursuit of knowledge the ethical issues raised by covert research are still open to debate. For instance we may plausibly argue that any citizen has the right to observe his fellows and to publish an account of what he sees, provided that he does not infringe their privacy. It makes no difference that the citizen in question has not been, say, a lathe operator all his life but is a social scientist who has put on dungarees temporarily in order to study rate-fixing and restriction of output. Likewise we may argue, provided we accept the validity of mental illness, that patients in a mental hospital are not fellow citizens with whom negotiation on a basis of equality is possible; by definition they are disenfranchised and may legitimately be deceived in their own true interests. I think that the first of these two arguments has some force but would not extend it to cover those instances where, for example, a social scientist is sponsored by the management of an enterprise to carry out covert research on its workers (cf. Bradney, 1957). Similarly it is interesting to note that Caudill, who first carried out covert research on mental hospital patients and then later made a similar study openly, reports that the data he gathered in the second study were equal in richness to those gathered covertly and that a high degree of control could be exercised over them (Caudill, 1958 : xv).

Social psychologists make considerable use of deception of another sort, in which the scientist does not conceal his identity but lies to the citizens. Asch's famous experiment on the perception of relative lengths, an investigation of the strength of pressures towards conformity, is an example of this kind of deception. In the experiment, seemingly honest volunteer college students were asked to state publically which of three lines on various cards matched in length a standard line on another card. In fact only one of the students was free to respond as he pleased. The other six or eight students answered according to instructions given to them beforehand. The object of the experiment was to discover to what extent the solitary 'critical' student, the naive subject in the jargon of the trade, clung to the evidence of his own eyes in the face of false testimony proclaimed by the stooges (Asch, 1956).

Misleading volunteer students about the relative lengths of lines on cards may seem harmless, particularly if, as in Asch's experiment, they are let into the secret afterwards. Innocence is open to question in the experiments on obedience carried out by Stanley Milgram (1974). Volunteer citizens were asked to administer electric shocks to an ostensible fellow citizen if he failed to answer various test questions correctly. The intensity of the shocks increased with continued failure. One of the objects of the experiment was to see whether the volunteers would administer shocks said to be sufficiently strong to be dangerous when required to do so by the rules of question and answer. An unexpectedly high proportion of volunteers did administer these dangerous shocks. In fact the individual receiving the shocks was a confederate or stooge, the shocks were imaginary and his screams of anguish were sham. The real anguish was generated in the minds of at least some of the volunteers who found themselves, in the context of the experiment, obeying orders to perform acts they normally would regard as reprehensible. These experiments have been extensively and heatedly discussed and the issues they raise are more complicated than I have indicated. The fact remains that Milgram was interested in discovering what circumstances were conducive to Eichmann-like behaviour in which individuals excuse themselves for acting cruelly by saying that they are acting under orders. To investigate this topic humanely, he had to mislead volunteers into thinking that their actions were cruel when in fact they were not.

Falling somewhere in between the types of deception practised by Asch and Milgram is the kind of duplicity used, for example, in Sissons' (1971) Paddington station experiment, in which unsuspecting travellers at Paddington railway station in London were asked by a stranger the way to Hyde Park. The encounter was filmed by a hidden camera and recorded on tape. After the stranger, who was in fact an actor working for Sissons, completed his encounter with the traveller, the latter was again accosted, this time by a research worker who explained that the traveller, unbeknown to himself, had just been taking part in an experiment and that he had been filmed and taped. The traveller was then asked various questions about himself so that his answers could be correlated with features of the encounter. Only one traveller out of eighty was indignant at being handled in this way; the others raised no objection. The object of the experiment was not to discover the best way to Hyde Park but to determine whether social class was associated with specified features of non-verbal communication with strangers. The success of the experiment clearly depended on the citizens remaining unaware that these features of their behaviour were under scrutiny. Thus citizens, who had not volunteered for this exercise, were put to some minor inconvenience in supplying information that was not needed in itself and, in the view of the solitary irate traveller, their privacy had been unjustifiably infringed by the filming and taping.

We see then that certain types of social inquiry require deliberate deception, at least initially, even if after the event the experimenter can let the citizens in on the plot, so that they can share with him in the joys of scientific discovery. The use of placeboes in double-blind clinical trials of new medicines involves a similar type of deception; the patient is given what the doctors hope he will believe are effective medicines when in fact they are not.

There are probably few people who would argue that deception in social inquiry, or indeed in clinical trials, is never ethically allowable. But several commentators have argued that Milgram was behaving unethically in conducting his obedience experiments, and it is easy to think of types of experimental deception that most or all of us would condemn. Even in a conventional ethnographic inquiry some deception may at times be necessary, as I discuss in the second lecture. If deception is sometimes justified in the name of science, what criteria should we use to determine which side of the line any given instance falls? More generally we may ask what considerations are relevant when the citizens under study are treated as somewhat less than fellow citizens, when the investigator does not negotiate with them as equals but assumes some kind of prior right to mislead them, invade their privacy and cause them inconvenience and maybe even temporary anguish.

Part of the answer to this difficult question will, I hope, emerge from the more detailed discussion of evidence that I attempt in the second and third lectures. A preliminary answer can be given in terms of the kind of society within which the interaction between investigator and citizen takes place.

Pluralist Society, Privacy and Sponsorship

We can begin by looking at two extreme cases. In a completely monolithic and totalitarian society the notions of privacy and private interest can scarcely find a place. If the true interests of each citizen are by definition identical with the interests of the state, and if social inquiry is an activity pursued only to further the interests of the state, then it follows that negotiations between the investigator and the citizens he studies are unnecessary and that any experimental deception that facilitates the successful outcome of the inquiry is perfectly permissible. At the other extreme we have the case of the absence of any common political or economic order linking the investigator and the citizens he studies, so that he has no power at all over them and has nothing to offer in negotiation. He can conduct his inquiries only in so far as they are prepared to tolerate his activities, for whatever reason. In real life neither extreme case is likely to occur, though some totalitarian regimes provide examples that approximate to one polar type and some instances of anthropological inquiries with previously uncontacted nomadic groups, for example Holmberg's work with the Siriono of Bolivia, carried out in the early 1940s (Holmberg, 1969), approximate to the other pole. Most real cases fall well towards the middle of the spectrum. Even where anthropologists are involved, there is usually some common social order to which the social scientists and the citizens both belong but where they have markedly divergent statuses and interests. The question is then the extent to which one side can or should put pressure on the other, and what benefits and advantages can be negotiated.

The notion of privacy gives us a rough and ready answer. Many cultures, probably most industrial and peasant cultures though perhaps not all tribal ones, recognize some distinction between public and private life, though they vary greatly in where the line is drawn between these two categories (Lee, 1948 : 394 ; Warner & Stone, 1970: 123–43). Within a given culture, the line may be drawn in different places according to context. In general, as a member of an organized community, certain of a citizen's attributes are public knowledge—his name and age, where he lives and so on. At the same time he has a recognized right, and even a duty, to keep hidden from public knowledge other attributes, notably his marital sexual activities. Other features of his life he may have to make known to the authorities but not necessarily to the public at large. For instance, in Britain, and I think in India too, information about a citizen's income and wealth falls into this intermediate category between public and private. The dividing line may be drawn differently for different classes of citizen, so that for so-called public figures more of their lives are made public knowledge than is the case with those citizens who live their lives in decent obscurity. Likewise those accused of crimes may find details of their private lives legitimately converted into public knowledge as a byproduct of the judicial process. Britain and Norway can serve to illustrate variations in where to draw the line. In Britain income tax-returns, although required of the citizen by law, are nevertheless regarded as so much part of private rather than public life that they do not become part of the national archives but are burnt after a number of years. On the other hand if a citizen is charged with driving a car while drunk, in Britain all his friends and neighbours will learn of the accusation by reading it in the local newspaper. By contrast, in Norway income-tax returns are perceived as one of the public aspects of citizenship in a democracy. Every year lists, showing the income of individuals and the tax each has to pay, are on display in local post offices. But if a Norwegian is arrested for drunken driving, his offence, even though it carries a mandatory jail sentence, is reported only anonymously in the press, so that his friends may never know about it.

Social inquiry often involves an invasion of the private sector of the lives of citizens. A good deal of research is, of course, carried out on documents all of which are already in the public domain. But as soon as an interviewer begins to ask about income, or political opinions, or voting behaviour, or even about preference for one breakfast cereal rather than another, he is in varying degrees invading the private domain of the citizens. To compensate for this intrusion, or to minimize its detrimental effect, the scientist can promise that the source of his information will not be made public, or he can pay for his information in money or in kind or by services rendered, or simply by being a patient listener. Citizens may welcome an opportunity to talk to a discreet and sympathetic stranger even on topics that are private. In practice, interviewers often try to justify a request for information by claiming that the authorities need to know in order to provide citizens with better social services, or that a manufacturer needs to know so that he may be able to market more attractive products. Likewise the field ethnographer may say that information on tribal customs is needed so that it can be recorded for the benefit of future generations of citizens. Some of these claims are more honest than others, but whatever argument is used the aim is at least to give the impression of negotiation as between equals. An alternative strategy is simply to assert that the government needs to know the facts, with the implication that government also knows what is best for the citizen and that he has no ground for complaint.

Thus it is typically when a plurality of diverse interests are recognized that serious ethical questions arise out of the relation between the inquiring social scientist and the citizen he studies. In a monolithic totalitarian society there is by definition no diversity of interest, while in the absence of any common framework linking scientist and citizen there is no basis for negotiation. Ethical questions about what information can be sought, what can be published, to whom in what form, what constraints one party may properly impose on the other—these questions arise only in connection with the process of negotiation between the parties. There is of course some room for ethical questions to arise even in the two ideal polar contexts that I have used as contrasts to the pluralist situation; but these questions are of a different order from those that arise in pluralist societies.

Our thesis that ethical questions in social inquiry arise mainly in pluralist societies is further supported when we consider the other major relation that sustains the process of inquiry, the relation between scientist and sponsor. In an ideal bureaucracy, as depicted by Max Weber, we have a micro-totalitarian part-society where there are rules in plenty but no ethical questions other than questions about the legitimacy of the rules themselves. If a social scientist is employed as a member of a bureaucracy, then in the ideal case he simply carries out his inquiries in accordance with the legitimate instructions of his superiors in the hierarchy. If he does not like the instructions, all he can do is resign. Luckily, Weberian ideal bureaucracies do not occur in real life. Nevertheless even a far-from-ideal bureaucracy poses special problems for a social scientist, particularly since his work necessarily involves him in evaluating the work of his colleagues in the bureaucracy, as Srinivas (1966: 161) points out with Indian government sociologists in mind. However rule-bound a real civil service may be, there will be conflicts of interest, displayed typically in the tension that exists between the civil service hierarchy and the professional organizations to which its specialist members belong (Brown, 1954).

Most of the non-routine forms of social inquiry, in most nations where social science is institutionalized, are carried out not by government employees but by other social scientists who are supported by some institution to which they are not bound body and soul. The supporting institution, the sponsor, has its own specific interests, which may range from a broad commitment to promote the pursuit of knowledge as an end in itself to an equally single-minded commitment to sell more breakfast foods. It might perhaps be thought that a body devoted to supporting pure research would provide funds without imposing any constraints on how the research is conducted. Even if this is sometimes the case, all such institutions must have criteria to enable them to make a rational choice among the numerous requests for their limited resources, and at least to this extent exercise an influence over the kind of research that is carried out. A sponsor supporting pure research may require that the research remains pure, that is, that there should be no immediate material payoff in sight. The sponsor is also likely to require a social scientist to report on one project before he receives support for the next. On the other hand a commercial organization, unless it is supporting pure research for reasons of publicity or altruism, is likely to specify fairly precisely what it wants to discover and how, if at all, the results of the inquiry shall be made public. The social scientist can then negotiate with his would-be sponsor to ensure that as far as possible his own interests in the research are secured. These may relate to the scope of the inquiry (for he may regard the specific information sought by his sponsor as merely incidental to some wider topic), the amount of freedom he shall have in deciding how the inquiry shall be conducted, and what form the report shall take. He may consider that he is obliged to protect his informants from his sponsor, particularly if they are acting illegally, and he may wish to protect his own professional interests by making sure that a full, fair and professionally acceptable report appears in print for the public. Professional reputations are made by publications, rather than by secret reports that colleagues cannot see.

In practice it is governments who provide most of the money for social research, and it is they who often endeavour to impose more binding constraints on the social scientist than do commercial sponsors. A government department often has complete control of access to unpublished official documents, and many departments have from time to time tried to extract a high price from the scientist for allowing him to see them. Departments that are not specifically committed to the pursuit of learning, such as those dealing with trade or housing, may consider that the public funds they can use to support research must be used for their own purposes, to secure data relevant to current departmental policies, rather than for the enhancement of learning and knowledge, and may therefore be less inclined to give the scientist a free hand than, for instance, are departments of education or science.

Many of the controversies that have arisen during the last twenty years or so over government sponsorship of social research have hinged on the use of money supplied by military departments. In an age of faith, if social science could then flourish, I am sure that similar controversies would arise over the use of funds supplied by departments of religious affairs. At the present time, for better or worse, these departments do not have large funds to disburse, whereas military departments are notoriously wealthy. Social scientists, as citizens, are more likely to be opposed, on grounds of politics or conscience, to the aims and ethos of military departments of governments than to the aims and policies of departments of housing and trade. This was particularly the case in the United States during the Vietnam war, and the ethical dilemmas that arose then were enhanced because for many years, particularly immediately after the end of the Second World War, American military departments had provided funds for many projects in social science that had no direct connection with any conceivable military objectives. For example, Asch's perception experiments, mentioned above, were financed by the United States Navy. During the Vietnam war the social scientist who was opposed to current military aims had to choose whether to reject the most likely source of support for his research or else to argue, as in Shaw's play *Major Barbara,* that money from an evil source diverted to good ends becomes money redeemed (Shaw, 1971:35–7)

Given, then, a plurality of sponsoring bodies, some taking the initiative in proposing specific topics for research and others waiting for requests for support from social scientist entrepreneurs, the way should be open for negotiation between sponsor and scientist just as, at either an earlier or later stage, there can be negotiation between scientist and citizens and, in some contexts, also with their gatekeepers. Ethical questions about how much the sponsor should interfere with the course of research, and how much autonomy the social scientist should retain—these questions arise in practice only when the would-be researcher is able to choose between possible sponsors, and when a would-be sponsor can choose which scientists to support for which projects. In particular these problems arise when the apparatus of government is sufficiently diversified and polycentric for its various agencies to have divergent and even conflicting aims. Shils (1956:235) describes pluralist societies as societies of privacy and publicity, which matches my own usage well, but it is more in terms of pluralist societies as characterized by a multiplicity of sources of power and influence and by a diversity of aims and values that ethical questions tend to arise in connection with social research. In these societies the resolution of ethical questions is a matter of practical and not merely philosophical importance. The same kinds of pluralist society give rise to parallel questions in the relation between the social scientist and the citizens he studies. The difficulties inherent in these questions are highlighted in the issues of deception and privacy. They arise in social science rather than in natural science because of that two-way interaction between scientist and citizen which is distinctive of social research. It is within the framework of this not-just-an-ideal model of a pluralist society, in which social science is an accepted and institutionalized part of culture, that I discuss more detailed contemporary and historical evidence in the two following lectures.

2

Ethical Problems in Practice

Sources

The principal components of our model of the process of social inquiry are social scientists, citizens, sponsors and gatekeepers. In this second lecture I apply this model to a few actual examples of social inquiry and comment on the ethical issues these examples raise. No one instance of social inquiry raises all possible interesting issues and therefore several cases are referred to.

When a book or monograph appears reporting the results of an empirical inquiry in social science, the author often says little about how he collected his data and less still about the ethical problems, if any, that he had to face during the various stages of his research. In those instances where these matters are discussed, the reader is in a better position to assess the report, to interpret its retentions and omissions and to be alert to its likely biases. One of the last phases of the process of inquiry, the impact of the published report on the sponsors, gatekeepers, scientists and, above all, the citizens whose lives are described, is likely to raise ethical questions, but these can be discussed only if and when a second edition of the report, or some supplement to it, is published. In addition to research reports there are a few collections of essays in which social scientists who have completed empirical inquiries and published their findings turn to reflect on how they went about their task, what political, ethical and technical problems they faced, where they went wrong and what they learnt from carrying out the research. These retrospective essays cover only a very small subset of all the empirical inquiries carried out in social science, but it is only from them, from the even smaller set of studies where the second edition of a report includes a discussion of how the first edition was received, and from the very few instances where a piece of research has be-come the subject of public controversy, that my examples are necessarily drawn.

The Wichita Jury Study : research and the public interest

My first case is taken from this last group of sources, where there has been public controversy. The preparation of a report and the repercussions of its publication often raise crucial ethical issues but in this inquiry the ethical and political issues were so acute that the study was never completed. The inquiry came to be known as the Wichita Jury Study and was carried out in 1954 as one part of a Univeisity of Chicago Jury Project. Microphones were installed in a courthouse in Wichita, in the United States, in the room in which the jury met to consider its verdict. During six civil cases, the deliberations of the jury were recorded on tape. The study was carried out by a team of researchers from the University of Chicago Law School as part of a larger inquiry into the American jury system and into various aspects of law observance and infringement. The whole inquiry was supported by a grant of four lakh dollars from the Ford Foundation. The research proposal put to the Foundation in 1952 referied in broad terms to study of the actual operation of the jury system; there was however no specific reference to any intention to record real jury deliberations, though the observation, under controlled conditions, of mock trials with selected juries was mentioned (cf. Broeder, 1959). Indeed, the suggestion that real jury delibcrations should be secretly recorded was first made in May 1953, nine months after the project had started, by a Wichita lawyer who had been circularized about the project. This lawyer proposed that recordings should be made only in civil and not in criminal cases, and that after the tapes of the deliberations had been transcribed they should be destroyed. The transcript should be edited to remove all personal names, geographical references and other identifying statements. The recordings were to receive no publicity until after the project had been completed.

Negotiation between the lawyer and local judges eventually led to a judge granting permission in February 1954 for recordings to be made in a limited number of cases, provided the counsel for each party agreed. The recordings were made without the knowledge and consent of the jurors. After six cases, recordings stopped.

In July 1955, for reasons for which the evidence is contradictory, an edited version of the deliberations of one of the juries was presented at the annual conference of lawyers associated with the court circuit in which the cases had been heard. The existence of the recordings thus became publically known and led to a public hearing by the Internal Security Subcommittee of the Committee on the judiciary of the United States Senate. Following the hearings, the senators concerned introduced a Bill which passed both Houses and came into effect in 1956. Under this Act, recording the deliberations of any federal jury for any purpose whatsoever is prohibited.

Both political and ethical issues are raised by this study. The political wish of the senators to discredit the sponsor, the Ford Foundation, and to discredit social science as well, led them to ignore the serious ethical issues which the inquiry brought to the surface. Following to some extent the analysis of the incident made by Vaughan (1967), we may contrast two ethical positions. On the one hand are those who argue that the citizen has an unalienable right to trial by an impartial jury, and that any violation of the privacy of a jury's deliberations puts its impartiality in jeopardy. Even though something of scientific or practical value might emerge from a scientific investigation of the operation of a jury during its deliberations, this could not outweigh the wrong done by compromising the opportunity to reach an impartial and just verdict. On the other hand are those who hold that knowledge is inherently superior to ignorance and that therefore there should always be unrestricted freedom of inquiry. It is socially and scientifically important to understand how the jury system works, and this understanding can be achieved only by direct investigation and observation of how it does in fact operate in real instances. The inquiry does not threaten the integrity of the jury system, for the scientist is not concerned with the actions of individual jurors but only with patterns of behaviour.

Clearly there are many intermediate ethical positions that may reasonably be taken; my own would fall well between the two I have contrasted. Nevertheless the two positions indicate the views taken respectively by the Senators and by some of the social scientists involved in the study.

In terms of our model, the citizens in this example are the members of the six juries, and their gatekeepers include the judges and counsel who gave permission for the deliberations to be recorded. The sponsor is the Ford Foundation and the scientists are a group drawn from the University of Chicago Law School, led by the Dean of the School, plus other lawyers who were drawn into the study. The two senators who conducted the hearings and later promoted the legislation that prevented any repetition of the inquiry do not fit easily into the model but may perhaps be regarded as additional self-appointed gatekeepers, anxious to shut the stable door even though six horses had already bolted.

First we should note that the gap between the two contrasted ethical positions is not simply a matter of conflicting ethical axioms, or of different orderings in a shared scale of values, but depends in part on a proposition that could be tested empirically, of at least in principle. It should be possible to discover, through mock trials, whether the verdicts reached by juries who are confident that their deliberations are not being recorded differ significantly from those reached by juries who know that they are being taped. If there is no difference, the social cost of the investigation is less, whereas if there is a significant difference the cost is greater. In my view, it would then be necessary for the scientists to provide stronger evidence that the information they seek is likely to lead to some improvement in the administration of justice, and that this information cannot be obtained by other means, for example from mock trials. Those who believe that there should be unrestricted freedom of scientific inquiry presumably would not agree with me.

The interests of the sponsor were involved in this case,both politically and ethically. The political issue, arising out of the connection, at this immediate post-McCarthy period, between the Ford Foundation and the University of Chicago, does not concern us here but we do have to consider the ethical issue of whether the Ford Foundation was misled about the kind of investigation for which it was providing ample financial support. Should the scientists conducting the project have informed the Foundation that, although it had not been envisaged in their original research proposal, they now intended to make recordings of actual jury deliberations? When they made a request for additional funds in December 1954, should they have mentioned that they had already made recordings and were currently engaged in editing them? They did not do so. In fact the Foundation approved an extension of the grant and voted additional funds just after the existence of the recordings had been made public. It seems therefore that from the viewpoint of the scientists nothing would have been lost had they taken the Foundation into their confidence about the recordings. Yet many scientists hold that it is their task, and theirs alone, to decide on the technical procedures to be followed in an inquiry and that a sponsor has no right to intervene in their area of professional expertise. But is the secret recording of a real jury carrying out its deliberations just a technical procedure of data collection?

The ethical issues salient in this incident, as Vaughan sets them out in his analysis, emerge from the falsely presumed conflict between a public interest in maintaining the integrity of the jury system and a scientific interest in discovering more about how that system operates, both as a contribution to knowledge and as the only sound basis for maintaining and improving the system. I find it interesting that Vaughan largely ignores what is surely an equally important ethical matter, whether or not the interests of the jurors were affected by the secret recordings of their deliberations. The Dean of the Law School argued during the hearings that if a juror was conscious that there was a microphone in the jury room, 'this might result in some inhibitions' (Vaughan, 1967: 62). The Dean presumably meant that the secret recording was somewhat similar to chose procedures of inquiry discussed in the first lecture, in which deception or secrecy is an intrinsic component,for if the citizen knows what is happening he will behave differently. Here there are two questions to ask. First, is it ethically or morally justifiable to allow a juror to think that he is not being recorded when in fact his words are being taped? Second, is the scientist justified in exposing the juror to the danger that what he says in the jury room, despite elaborate precautions about security of tapes and thoroughness in editing, may still become public knowledge in some more or less identifiable form? After Watergate, even the most earnest advocate of the freedom of scientific inquiry may be allowed to hesitate before answering yes to the second question, even if he can dispose of the first more easily.

One final point can be made about the Wichita Jury Study. Even if everything had gone according to plan and there had not been a premature disclosure of the existence of the tapes, the book that was envisaged as an outcome of the inquiry would necessarily have revealed to the general public that somewhere in America, at some recent point in time, recordings had been made of actual jury deliberations. I cannot believe that the edited transcripts would have been used merely as background briefing for the scientists, and that their existence could have been kept secret permanently. Yet once it became known that recordings had been made, then any potential juror could expect that the experiment might be repeated on him. Indeed, given the competitive climate of research, and the methodological stress on the merits of replication, the pressure to repeat the inquiry would have been very strong. Thus a permanent change in the jury system would have been made, provided that, as both the Senators and the Dean appeared to have believed, jurors who know that they are being taped do in fact behave differently from those who are confident that they are not. The social scientists seem to me to have acted irresponsibly in not considering the consequences of this inevitable change, and also in not trying to discover empirically whether the change would be beneficial or harmful or insignificant. As it happened, the only change that occured was legislation that precluded any further inquiry of this kind. The legislation was prompted much more by political considerations, by the desire to discredit social science and to protect traditional American social institutions from rational scrutiny, than from any consideration of ethical issues.

The Wichita jury study throws no light on what happens when scientist and citizen interact over a long period, or on the consequences of publication. It does however provide us with a good example of how ethical and political issues become intertwined, and of how gatekeepers can intervene to modify and even, as in this case, to halt the progress of research.

The Glacier Project : the scientist as clinician

The next inquiry is marked by the careful attention paid by the scientists to the interests of the citizens. In the Glacier Project a factory in north-west London was studied for several years by a team of research workers belonging to the Tavistock Institute of Human Relations. Relations between scientists and sponsor in this inquiry seem not to have been important; indeed it is not clear from the published reports who the sponsor was. We are told only that the grant was administered by the (United Kingdom) Medical Research Council, a body whom the author of the main report on the project describes as 'disinterested'. The study was endorsed by the Council for Industrial Productivity.

We are however told a good deal about relations between scientists and citizens. At the time of the study the Institute undertook consultancy work in addition to carrying out research on its own initiative. In both types of activity it was heavily committed to combining scientific inquiry with ameliorative action, and was popularly credited with the slogan: 'No research without therapy, no therapy without research.' Much of its work was carried out on industry. Requests for advice as consultants inevitably came from the managements of industrial enterprises rather than from, say, committees of shop stewards or individual employees. Nevertheless the Institute followed a policy of refusing on principle any request for consultation that did not have the agreement of representatives of the workers as well as of management. In the Glacier case, the initial approach was made by a research team of the Institute, rather than by the Glacier management. Three months of negotiation were needed before the quick positive response from the management was matched by an expression of approval from the committee of workers' representatives. This endorsement was secured only after the Trades Union Congress and the relevant trade union confederation had both been persuaded to give the proposed research their imprimatur. These bodies were, in our terms, invoked as protective gatekeepers by the workers' representatives who were initially suspicious of what appeared to them as merely the latest gimmick of management. Once the research team and its objective had been approved by management and workers, its members carefully specified what role they should play in the factory. An agreed statement of their position was posted on notice-boards in the factory, announcing that the team would act only in an advisory or interpretative capacity; that when an individual or group suggested a topic for study by the research team, it would be looked at only with the general approval of those likely to be affected by the results; and that nothing would be done behind anyone's back, that is, that no issue would be discussed unless representatives of the group were present or had agreed to the topic being raised.

Here then we have a striking instance of social scientists taking explicit steps to protect what they perceive as being the diverse interests of the citizens they are studying. The model they tried to follow was taken from clinical medicine, with its careful delineation of what constitutes professional conduct. In their efforts to avoid appearing to favour one group in the factory rather than another and, as they put it, to prevent themselves being captured by any particular group, they limited their contacts with members of the factory to strictly formal contexts and steadfastly refused to be drawn into any extra-professional ties. They refused invitations to play tennis, or to attend parties or to do anything that, as it were, might involve them as ordinary human beings interested in fellow citizens, since such interaction would necessarily conflict with their impartial research role. Thus their mode of inquiry was as far removed as possible from participant observation, where the inquirer seeks to broaden the scope of his observations by participating in the various activities carried on by the citizens.

One other important consequence of the high value placed on professional impartiality is seen in the procedure adopted for publications. The research team undertook, apparently on its own initiative, not to make any public statement about the project except in collaboration with the firm or after due consultation. The book, *The Changing Culture of a Factory*, by Elliot Jaques (1951), which was the first major publication to emerge from the study, was treated as one of these public statements. Consequently each section of the book was circulated in draft to, and discussed in detail with, each of the groups particularly concerned. The book as a whole was then vetted by the Works Council, the main meeting-place of management and workers. Jaques' comment on this procedure is particularly interesting for the light it throws on the research team's perception of balanced interests and of its commitment to therapy as well as to research. Jaques writes :

> . . . it being assumed that where the work of the project was successful in assisting the resolution of group problems there would be no difficulty in publication; and conversely, any differences arising over publication would indicate that the problems on which assistance had been sought were insufficiently worked-through, and, hence, were not ready to be written up [Jaques 1951:16].

Thus in this project explicit and almost self-conscious attention was paid to the interests of citizens. The study exposes strikingly the basic tenet of the human relations school of management (Baritz, 1960), of which the Tavistock Institute is one of the chief supporters. The researchers recognized the existence of a diversity of interest among the citizens, in this case between management and workers, and between various groups of management and workers, and took elaborate measures to institutionalize this diversity. But at the same time they acted on the premise that conflicts arising from a divergence of interest could, in the end, be resolved by some quasi-clinical procedure of discussion and working-through, as if the factory were a patient stretched on the couch of a psycho-analyst. It is, of course, just for this reason that the human relations school has been attacked by Marxists and others who hold that differences of interest between economic classes are too fundamental to be resolved by discussion with a clinically-clad member of a research team.

In the Glacier study we can see how an ethical stance taken by social scientists can determine how topics are selected for inquiry, how they are studied and how they are reported on to the public. It is easier for a research institute, with an ongoing programme of research extending over the years, to publicize and maintain a distinctive ethical code than it is for a single research worker to do so. Nevertheless, individual researchers each have their own ethical and political commitments and, though these may be harder to identify, they may have just as great an effect on research procedures, and on the unstated assumptions underlying their reports.

As far as I know, no information is available about what effect, if any, publication of *The Changing Culture of a Factory* had on the Glacier factory, even though reports on further studies carried out there by the Institute have appeared. It would be interesting to discover whether or not the publication of the way in which problems were satisfactorily 'worked through' and resolved was for all concerned quite as peaceful as Jaques implies that it would be.

Street Corner Society : the limits of participation

I have chosen for my next example a study in which, as in the Glacier Project, a good deal of attention was paid to the wording of the final report but where the mode of data collection differed radically from that followed in the Glacier study, and where the range of ethical issues raised was greater.

Whyte's *Street Corner Society* (1955) is a study of a slum area of Boston inhabited mainly by Italian immigrants to the United States. The study was carried out just before the Second World War, and the book that emerged from it has become a classic. Here, just as in the Glacier Project, the sponsor of the research was disinterested, for the Society of Fellows of Harvard University gave Whyte a very free hand. At several points in his study Whyte, rather than his sponsor, became concerned about his association with Harvard University, particularly when he feared that he might be arrested for illegal activities. He says that he resolved that if he was caught he would not mention his connection with the University. This device of protecting the fair name of a sponsor by concealing one's link with it is unlikely to apply in most contexts.

In this study there were no gatekeepers, though initially Whyte found it difficult to establish the personal relations he sought with the residents of the slum. He eventually made contact, through a social worker attached to a settlement house, with a man called Doc, who later became his principal informant and assistant. It is interesting that the only segment of the community that subsequently objected to Whyte's report was the social workers. They considered that Whyte had betrayed them, apparently because the book makes it clear that the 'corner boys', the groups of mainly unemployed young men who form the focus of Whyte's study, were scarcely being helped at all by the activities of social workers. In his fieldwork, once having met Doc, Whyte rapidly made contacts with members of the community and ceased to be associated with the settlement house. When he left Boston after three and a half years fieldwork, a farewell beer party was held for him, organized not by the settlement house but by a recreational club he had joined. Some writers on field methods argue that a fieldworker ought to extricate himself from a field situation by the same route as he entered it, in this way making manifest his obligation to those who have facilitated his entry and at the same time indicating that the special status he has claimed for himself as a field investigator is being terminated. Such a procedure may well be appropriate, and even unavoidable, in studying a formally structured and protected community like a factory or a tribe living on a reserve, but seems less necessary where the community is an urban slum, open to anyone, and where the investigator is a fellow citizen from a university only two or three miles away. In any case, for reasons that Whyte sets out in his retrospective account of his fieldwork, social workers in the slum are likely to have been upset by his account of their shortcomings however carefully he might have tried to negotiate his withdrawal with them (cf. Whyte, 1941).

In his book, Whyte disguises the identity of the individuals whose actions are recorded, and even disguises the location of the study. Boston appears in the book as 'Eastern City'. He says that he did this to avoid embarrassment to the individuals concerned. Although some of these individuals were engaged in illegal activities which are described, it is not the exposure of these that Whyte had in mind nor, indeed, what his informants disliked. The citizens with whom

Whyte discussed the text of his book disliked being described in their true colours, warts and all, even under disguised names. 'The trouble is, Bill, you caught the people with their hair down. It's a true picture, yes; but people feel it's a bit too personal.' On the other hand his main informant, Doc, told him, 'This will embarrass me, but this is the way it was, so go ahead with it'. Whyte himself, however, seems to have been more concerned that those members of a gang who ranked low in the hierarchy of prestige and power would be embarrassed to see in print how low they ranked and the sorts of difficulties they got into because of this.

In stressing embarrassment at the documentation of low status and at the publication of acts done when, as it were, the citizens were not on their best behaviour, rather than at the exposure of illegal acts, Whyte adopts an attitude of moral relativism. This attitude may be easy to take when, for example, an anthropologist studies a tribal society with a code of moral and ethical values differing dramatically from his own, but it is harder to sustain when the citizens under study are indeed legally fellow citizens and near neighbours in the same urban conurbation. Whyte takes the ethical code of the slum as unproblematic for members of the slum, yet expresses a good deal of anxiety when, as a marginal member of the slum community, he himself is led to break the law. Part of this anxiety sprung from the fear of being caught, and of involving the repute of his academic sponsors, but part arises from the moral conflict he experienced. He describes vividly how he became involved in 'repeating', that is, voting several times in an election in other voters' names. Analysing this experience, he says that he was wrong to go against his conscience. He says 'I had to learn that, in order to be accepted by the people in a district, you do not have to do everything just as they do it. . . . I also had to learn that the fieldworker cannot afford to think only of learning to live with others in the field. He has to continue living with himself.'

In my view, this is sound advice, but it raises the question of the extent to which a fieldworker's own code of ethics can diverge from that held by the citizens with whom he works. In Whyte's case not everyone indulged in 'repeating', and those who did 'were generally looked down upon as the fellows who did the dirty work'. It would therefore have been acceptable in the eyes of the slum community for Whyte to have refused to 'repeat'. On the other hand, Whyte felt no obligation to report to the police other instances of law-breaking that he saw going on around him. Indeed, it seems that under Massachusetts law, he had no legal liability to take the initiative in doing so (Broeder, 1960 : 71–2, 88 ; cf. Brymer Farris, 1967; 312–13). Had he considered it his duty to inform the police, he could scarcely have carried out his study. More serious dilemmas of the same kind arise whenever social scientists carry out field studies of juvenile delinquency and other forms of criminal activity, and are known to possess information about crimes that are still being investigated by the police.

Whyte's carefully analysed retrospective doubts about 'repeating', and his acquiescence in other instances of law-breaking, contrast strikingly with the attitude taken by another social scientist who, while working in a tribal area of his own country, was invited to agree that a senile woman should be buried alive. Several decades after the event, he baldly reports that 'Of course I agreed', though he excused himself from being present when the deed was done (Hart, 1970 : 154).

These reports suggest that, whether or not fieldworkers and their professional colleagues adhere to dogmas of cultural and ethical relativism, there has to be a fairly high degree of compatibility between the ethical codes held by social scientists and the citizens they select for study. It is, for instance, unlikely that a social scientist who is a pacifist could establish empathic relations with an active military group (cf. Daniels, 1967), or that one who believes that the Pope is anti-Christ could gain rapport with a community of Catholic monks.

To some extent any scientist working in the field finds himself in the position described by Beteille (1975)in the context of his contacts with Harijans in a village in Tamilnadu in which he deliberately chose to identify himself with the resident Brahmins. His hosts and neighbours objected to Harijans coming to visit him at his house and he therefore changed his mode of contact with them. He writes of his Brahmin neighbours : '. . . if I was to be given access to their homes and temples—to which access was not given easily to outsiders—I could not violate their sentiments at will'. These issues are, of course, partly matters of field tactics rather than of ethics but obviously the extent to which a fieldworker can bring himself to conform to the value-system of the citizens, or maybe on occasion consciously to violate the tenets of that system, depends in part on the relation between the local value system and the system of values held by the fieldworker in his capacity as a citizen. I agree with Dube (1973 : 20) when he says, 'The "social scientist" and the "citizen" cannot be compartmentalized; it is not possible for a citizen having personal values to bring about an instant role-switch, immunize himself to value-virus, and start functioning as an ethically neutral social scientist'.

In the same way there must be some compatibility between the views of the scientist and his sponsor. As Orlans (1967:5) puts it bluntly: '. . . if you disagree with the objectives of an agency [i.e. sponsor] don't decry the morality of its staff, but try to change their objectives and, in the interim, don't take their money.'

Whyte raises another ethical point when he discusses his role as participant observer, and adopts a viewpoint that, rather surprisingly in view of the difference in their styles of work, matches that taken by the Glacier research team. Starting from the premise that the interests of the citizens must be respected, the Glacier investigators assert that 'any action for research purposes alone without regard to the needs of the client would be regarded as a breach of the professional role of the research worker' (Wilson, 1951 : xv). Whyte discusses how he spoke in support of a proposal at a political meeting merely in order to get himself into closer contact with a prominent racketeer. The manoeuvre failed for, feeling sure of Whyte's support, the racketeer ignored him. Whyte says, 'Here I violated a cardinal role of participant observation. I sought actively to influence events. . . . it had . . . been a violation of professional ethics. It is not fair to the people who accept the participant observer for him to seek to manipulate them to their possible disadvantage, simply in order to seek to strengthen his social position in one area of participation.' If we adopt Whyte's view, then all field experimentation is ruled out, or at least all experimentation with significant consequences. Indeed, it is difficult to reconcile Whyte's assertion that a participant observer should never attempt to influence the course of events with his own action in connection with the public bathhouse in the slum. There was no hot water and Whyte decided that something should be done to improve matters. He says, 'I tried to tell myself that I was simply testing some of the things I had learned about the structure of corner gangs, but I knew really that this was not the main purpose'. Whyte then goes on to describe, with approval, how he organized a partially successful march on Boston city hall to demand hot water. The correct analysis is, I think, not that a professional ethic requires a participant observer never to intervene—something indeed which would conflict with the whole notion of participation. It is rather that intervention that does not lead to, or does not at least responsibly aim at, some enhancement of the interests of the citizens most directly affected by the intervention is necessarily suspect. The Tavistock formulation seems sounder to me than Whyte's.

Kashmiri Pandits : scientist or fellow citizen?

Another good example of respect for the interests of citizens is provided by the work of T.N. Madan among Kashmiri Pandits. He (1975) has described how as a graduate student he was taken on a fieldwork training trip entailing two weeks of inquiry among Oraons living near Ranchi. For him this was a depressing and even traumatic experience, for he was upset by the behaviour of his fellow students. He says 'Everyone was asking the people questions about their most intimate relationships and fondest beliefs, without any regard for their feelings or convenience. . . . I had the uncomfortable feeling that there was something indecent about such a field trip.' Later, when he went to study citizens of his own community living in Kashmir, he was expected to abide by the basic rules of social, moral and ritual conduct prevalent among the citizens. They accepted him as a rather wayward Pandit now engaged on a special task of social inquiry, and at the same time accepted the role of informants for themselves. Although the citizens were at first unwilling to talk to him about confidential matters, he was gradually able to gather information about a wide range of topics. Nevertheless many Pandits tried to shift this role allocation and attempted to absorb Madan into village life where, in their view, he properly belonged. After a while he was asked to intervene in family disputes over property and thus gained access to information about conflicts, a topic that he had hitherto found very difficult to investigate. He says that he was then faced with the ethical problem of what use he might make of information acquired in this way, and says that some of the information in his possession he decided not to publish, even though it was relevant to the theme of his book (Madan, 1965: 12). Had the village he studied been hidden under a pseudonym, and its location obscured, then Madan might have had to decide how impenetrable a disguise he should employ before he could justifiably make use of the information. The ethical issue was, I think, simplified for him by the citizens' insistence that the identity of their village should not be disguised at all.

Zuni : passing on information

Madan was himself a Pandit and it is therefore not surprising that the Pandits he studied should judge him by their own standards. Yet any fieldworker who 'lives intimately with strangers', to use Madan's vivid expression, will sooner or later be judged by the citizens in their own terms, however alien he may be to them. Thus, for example, Berreman, an American who worked in India, reports a citizen saying to him, 'You may be a foreigner and we only poor villagers, but when we get to know you we will judge you as a man among other men: not as a foreigner' (Berreman, 1972: xxvi).

One aspect of being judged as a man among other men that every fieldworker has to come to terms with, whether he is working among citizens like himself or among people with radically different customs and values, is to what extent he should pass on to other members of the community the information he collects in the course of his inquiries. This may seem to be a straightforward matter but the available evidence shows that there is no simple formula that can be applied in all cases. Some field ethnographers have stated that they endeavoured to respect the confidence placed in them by their informants and therefore considered that they should not pass on to other members of the community any information collected in the ethnographer-informant context. Some have reported that only by being seen to be reticent in this way were they able to establish reputations as men of integrity. This has been my own experience in the field (cf. Berreman, 1972 : xlvi - lvi). Yet T.N. Pandey, whose account of fieldwork among the Zuni of the United States shows a sensitive awareness of the ethical issues in his relations with citizens, reports that he always told the old woman in whose house he lived what he had learned from different sources. He says 'Zuni Indians resented their favourite anthropologists working with anyone outside the narrow family circle'. They were afraid of being suspected of disclosing tribal secrets, and felt unsafe if 'their' anthropologist went to talk to someone who might spread a rumour that they had done so. Therefore when Pandey talked to someone with whom his hosts were not on good terms, he was often asked on his return what had been said about them (Pandey, 1975 : 200, 210). The Zuni are well-known for their highly developed sense of privacy, and for their sharp dichotomization of information into public and secret, and it would seem that Pandey was expected not to keep information secret from his hosts. Nevertheless, I find it surprising to learn that the topics in which Pandey was interested were factionalism and in-group hostility, and attitudes towards envy, gossip, slander and hate. Presumably it was information bearing on these topics that he recapitulated to his hostess, apparently on his own initiative. We may perhaps infer that at least in those areas of discourse with which Pandey was concerned, Zuni draw a socio-centred rather than an ego-centred dividing line between public and secret topics. Although the sanctions against disclosure of group secrets to non-members are stricter among the Zuni than in many other societies, in the public domain there is freedom to collect information for all approved inquirers.

But however the notions of privacy, secrecy and publicity may be defined and delimited in particular cultures, the onward transmission of information collected in the course of fieldwork is likely always to raise questions of ethics, whatever the culture and whether the information concerns illegal activities, political manoeuvres, marital intrigues, idle gossip or even issues that are fully public knowledge. The social scientist, even if he shelters behind a clinical white coat as in the Glacier case, cannot be simply a sink or sponge, soaking up information and never transmitting any. He must have something to offer in return. Presumably in all cultures some kinds of information are public enough to be passed on with impunity. In the case of a scientist studying a community far removed from his own, he is the potential source of information about his own society that may be fresh and interesting to the citizens. I think that it is legitimate to avoid expatiating in this context on those aspects of one's own society that may be intellectually incomprehensible or morally offensive to the citizens concerned—for example, the contemporary indifference to marriage in many Western societies. Yet it seems to me both unnecessary and wrong to convey false information, as has sometimes been done. For example, Bateson (1958 : 232) explained a lunar eclipse, to an informant who had told him that the sun was a cannibal, by ascribing the redness of the moon to blood in the sun's excrement which had come between the earth and the moon.

Hindus of the Himalayas : telling all or only some?

In my last example I take up again the topic of deception discussed in the first lecture, but now with reference to inquiries carried out in the field rather than in the morally specialized environment of a psychological laboratory. In what circumstances and to what extent may a scientist mislead the citizens as to what he is really doing when he interacts with them?

This question arises inescapably where deception is achieved by some positive misleading act as in many laboratory experiments, but is also present, if not so salient, when the deception takes the form of an act of omission. Although the scientist may reasonably be expected to convey to the citizens his broad research goals, does he have to specify in detail what hypotheses he seeks to test, or what particular topics he would like to concentrate upon? He must be reasonably honest with the citizens; must he be absolutely honest? Positive acts of deception occur typically in psychological research, whereas in the course of intensive and extended field research typical of social anthropology and sociology, the scientist is more likely to find himself misleading the citizens by remaining silent about the main focus of his research interests. This happens not merely because of the intellectual or cognitive gap between him and them to which I referred in the first lecture; it also arises particularly during that first traumatic period at the beginning of a field study, when the incoming scientist is still perceived as a potentially dangerous stranger and while the citizens are still very curious to discover whether he is a spy, missionary, policeman or merely a harmless academic. To state bluntly at this early stage in the encounter that he has come to study, say, the mechanisms of factionalism, the sanctions against rate-busting, the incidence of adultery, or the extent of religious heterodoxy may be just as disasterous, from the point of view of achieving the objectives of the research, as it is to explain in advance the true aim of psychological tests. How honest, then, does the scientist have to be with the citizens?

The most perceptive analysis of this ethical question that I have seen is that provided by Berreman who, in effect, argues that the scientist does not need to be more open and honest with the citizens than they are with one another and with him. His analysis is based on the distinction made by Goffman (1969 : 92–122) between back and front regions of social space. The back region is where the social actors prepare themselves in secret for the public performances they enact in the front region. The sociologist is, as Srinivas (1966 : 156) says, 'like a novelist who must of necessity get under the skin of the different characters he is writing about'. Yet whereas he tries to find out what is really going on behind the scenes in the back region, the citizens are, atleast initially, anxious that he should observe them only on the public performances of their social roles. In Whyte's terms, they don't like being seen with their hair down. In Berreman's view, the scientist, or the research team to which he belongs, likewise divide their activities between front and back regions. Writing of his work as an anthropologist in Uttar Pradesh he says, 'the ethnographer will be presenting himself in certain ways to his informants during the research and concealing other aspects of himself from them. They will be doing the same. This is inherent in all social interaction.' Given this interpretation of what happens in practice, he says, 'I believe it to be ethically unnecessary and methodologically unsound to make known his specific hypotheses and in many cases his area of interest. To take his informants into his confidence regarding these may well preclude the possibility of acquiring much information essential to the main goal of understanding their way of life' (Berreman, 1972:xxxiv). In Berreman's case one of his main foci of interest was inter-caste relations, yet his initial presentation of his interests to the citizens was in terms of America's need to learn more about India following her achievement of Independence, and of the increasing role that the inhabitants of the Himalayan region would play in the independent nation (Berreman, 1972: xxv).

I accept the validity of Berreman's model of social interaction but I think that he does not entirely settle the ethical question. Indeed, he seems to put forward his answer as appropriate merely in those contexts, like the one in which he worked, where ascription, i.e. caste membership by birth, is the only criterion for full acceptance in the society. He leaves unstated whether or not his normative pronouncement applies to other situations where the relation between scientist and citizens is not constrained in this way. My own view is that the extent to which the scientist should take the citizens into his confidence depends at any time on the extent to which he has established relations of mutual trust and sympathy with them, and on the degree of congruence between their cognitive and affective views of the world and his. It may be harmless enough to begin an inquiry into some controversial topic like wife-swapping or illegal distilling by professing to be interested only in a general understanding of how the citizens live. Nevertheless the scientist should try to communicate to the citizens a deeper and constructive appreciation of what his research is really aimed at. The sooner he does this the better, and the more likely that trouble will be avoided when he publishes his report on the research.

Yet perhaps this pious advice is unnecessary. Berreman's book describes how Brahmins and Rajputs sacrifice animals, eat meat, drink alcohol, ignore the great Hindu gods, marry widows, marry across caste lines, are polygynous and polyandrous, and sell women to men from the plains (Berreman, 1972 : xxxviii–xxxix). Despite this catalogue of enormities, his book was apparently perceived by the citizens as not disparaging their mountain village, and its publication did not result in any attention being paid to their village by policeman, government agents or missionaries. Accordingly, when Berreman returned ten years later, they were glad to welcome him back (Berreman, 1972: 367). Hence it appears that not only was it tactically expedient for Berreman to remain initially silent about his research objectives, but that no deleterious consequences for the citizens or for him resulted from his silence. Thus again we see that the distinctive features of a field situation may play havoc with standardized ethical prescriptions.

Conclusions

The examples used in this lecture do not display the full range of ethical issues that arise in connection with empirical inquiry in social science. In particular little has been said about relations with sponsors and gatekeepers, and about the consequences of publication. But these examples, which, as we should expect, all come from pluralist societies, should be sufficient to give some indication of how wide this range is. Though I have indicated some of the likely ethical questions, I have done little to supply correct answers to them. Indeed it should be clear that these issues cannot be resolved easily by reference to any detailed standard code. Part of the difficulty that many professional bodies have experienced in trying to draw up a code of ethics (cf. Unnithan, *et al.*, 1967 : 185–9) springs from the diversity of ethical positions held by their members, but part comes from the great variety of social and cultural contexts in which empirical research is carried out. The counsels of perfection that may be appropriate and applicable when a social scientist studies citizens similar to himself, with the same values and assumptions, and similarly placed in relation to power and resources, may be inappropriate and inapplicable when there is a great cultural gap between the parties or where there is a great disparity, one way or the other, between them in terms of power to articulate and defend their interests. In each case we can go back to first principles and endeavour to see to what extent the commitment to the pursuit of knowledge, which is the diacritical mark of the scientist, can be reconciled with the short-term and long-term interests of sponsors, citizens and the wider public who may benefit or be harmed by the outcome of the inquiry.

One reason why the examples presented in this lecture may give the impression that no generalizations can be made about what should or should not be done is that I have treated them all in a historical terms, without reference to the historical circumstances in which they are embedded. Taking the historical context into account does not magically resolve all ethical questions, but it does introduce a new dimension in terms of which some regularity and consistency begins to emerge. Further examples in an historical and developmental context are given in the third lecture.

3
Social Science in a Post-imperial World

The Age of Positivism and the Natural Science Paradigm

I began my first lecture by contrasting the social sciences with the natural sciences and the humanities. This third lecture is organized around another contrast, between the social sciences at three points of time: first as they emerged in recognizable form in the middle of the nineteenth century, then as they were practised in the 1930s when capitalism and imperialism still enjoyed widespread confidence, and finally as they are today, when imperialism in its classic mode has greatly diminished and when capitalism, while in no sense disappearing from the world, is at least undergoing a major transformation. With the help of this tripartite contrast I hope to throw some light on the ethical dilemmas discussed in the second lecture.

For our present purposes we must treat the complex historical development of the social sciences quite cavalierly and simply say that interest in economics and sociology grew in response to the process of industrialization in Western Europe and North America, whilst social anthropology constituted a similar response to the problems raised by imperialism. All three disciplines began to establish themselves during the nineteenth century though, as Srinivas and Panini (1973 : 181-2) point out, in India the importance of collecting local ethnographic information was recognized by the Governor of Bengal and Bihar as early as 1769.

As an empirical science, nineteenth century economics relied heavily, as the discipline still does today, on data collected by government agencies. Sociologists, with an interest in many topics lying outside the systematic concern of governments, had perforce to collect most of their own data. As early as 1834 the Statistical Society of London drew up questionnaires, or 'interrogatories' as they were then called, in order to collect information on the condition of the poor, strikes and similar topics (Abrams, 1968 : 18). A few years later the Society undertook field surveys of particular communities, again with an interest in the concomitants of poverty. Thus the widely circulated questionnaire and the local study in depth, the two main modes of social inquiry even today, were adopted from the start. The focus of attention was industrialization and its evil effects—overcrowding, low wages, poor working conditions, strikes, prostitution, urban drunkenness. Inquiries into these topics were undertaken in the expectation that once the existence of bad conditions had been demonstrated, the government or private bodies could be persuaded to take effective ameliorative action. Even theorizing at the most abstract level, as exemplified in the writings of Auguste Comte, was linked to programmes of political action, mainly of a conservative character. Outside the main stream of academic sociology, Karl Marx, who is now canonized as one of its founding fathers, was advocating political action of a very different type.

It is not surprising that during this period little attention was paid to ethical questions. There was a wide social gulf between the elite who organized the inquiries and the unfranchised working class about whom they inquired. The social action which it was hoped would follow from the results of the inquiries was action to be taken by the elite, or its agents, acting on the pauper, the drunkard and the criminal. There was no concept of negotiation with fellow citizens, for the true interests of the working class were defined for them by their social superiors. Thus, for example, in the very first paper to be published in the *Journal of the Statistical Society of London* in 1838, where a proposal was made to establish special schools for the children of paupers, the author stated that 'The great object to be kept in view in regulating any school for the instruction of the children of the labouring class, is the rearing of hardy and intelligent working men, whose character and habits shall afford the largest amount of security to the property and order of the community' (Kay, 1838 : 23; cf. Abrams, 1968 : 22). This autocratic attitude towards the definition of the interests of the people whose lives were being investigated was reinforced by the positivistic faith that the true facts of poverty, or of any other social phenomenon, existed in some absolute and objective sense and were waiting only to be discovered by unbiased investigators.

If ethical considerations did not impinge on the process of social inquiry in the metropolitan country, it is only to be expected that they would be ignored by anthropologists operating overseas. For if sociology in the early nineteenth century may be said to have been in harmony with the interests of the rising bourgeoisie, anthropology, both in theory and practice, allied itself more closely with the interests of the aristocracy, particularly in Britain. This linkage still endures, as for example in the choice of the Prince of Wales as patron of the Royal Anthropological Institute in London. Despite this difference in alignment, both sociology and anthropology were elitist rather than populist. Anthropology took over the explanatory framework of the most prestigious natural science of the time, geology, and transformed its natural history approach into a theory of social evolution. Later, at the very end of the nineteenth century, the methodology of physics and of Francis Bacon, lately brought up to date by John Stuart Mill, was applied to anthropological fieldwork in a positivist spirit. In one of the first important anthropological field expeditions, the Cambridge Anthropological Expedition to Torres Straits, we find reproduced in a tropical colonial setting the same conditions for investigation as we might have found at that time in a physical laboratory. The main difference was that the objects being investigated were not molecules but natives. The scientists were like men from Mars, qualitatively different from the non-citizens they had come half-way round the world to study. Although in fact the scientists were fellow human beings, and in a limited domestic sense had to interact with the natives in this capacity, this interaction is rigidly excluded from the formal reports of the expedition. Indeed, all we know about how Haddon and his fellow scientists lived in the field is derived from Haddon's popular account (1901) and a biography by his pupil (Quiggin, 1942: 95-108). Apart from one historical chapter and two brief descriptions of the system of administration imposed by the Queensland government, the six volumes that eventually constituted the record of the expedition's findings attempt to convey information about how the natives acted and talked in their pristine state, before becoming contaminated by contacts with missionaries, pearlers and other Australians. The reports themselves (Cambridge Anthropological Expedition 1901-1935) appeared up to thirty-six years after the expedition had returned to Britain and were published there rather than in Australia. They were clearly not designed to have any practical implications, either for the natives or for the Queensland administration which had assumed control over so many of their activities.

I have cited the Torres Straits expedition because it is well known but the conditions under which the members of that expedition went about their work, and the conceptual framework in which they made their inquiries, are typical of a good deal of early anthropological inquiry. Fieldworkers varied greatly in the extent to which they merely asked formal questions and collected verbatim texts, or, on the other hand, participated wholeheartedly in the activities of the people they were studying, but in terms of research design they all followed the same natural-science paradigm. The people were to be studied as they would have been but for the disturbing effects introduced by the presence of the fieldworkers and often of missionaries, traders, recruiters and administrators as well. These disturbances did not form part of the field of study (cf. Haddon, 1935 : xiv), and preferably were to be kept to a minimum; hence the well-known preference for studying so-called 'untouched' tribes. The natives supplied information in a one-way process, and once the data had been collected, they played no further part. Data analysis was something that concerned the scientist alone, and publication was for the benefit of scholars everywhere, rather than for the peoples whose lives were described. By and large anthropologists, like their sociological colleagues, were positivists. Their basic premise that there were true facts that could be discovered by inquiry was not affected by the exotic context in which they worked. Nor later was it shaken by the expansion of the positivistic rubric to include the attitudes and feelings of the individuals being studied, as advocated by Max Weber and Malinowski.

In one minor respect anthropologists paid heed to considerations of privacy. Some of the behaviour they observed in the field, or about which they were told, was considered to be offensive to Western tastes and was therefore reported not in English, French or German but in Latin. This was, of course, a concession to the susceptibilities not of the natives but of European readers, who were spared a forced confrontation with unpleasant sexual activities but who could, if they wished, savour the facts in a properly clinical context. The use of Latin also ensured that these exotic facts were confined to the elite and did not diffuse among the lower orders of society, who might misapply them.

During this first period the dominant characteristic of the relation between the scientist and the not-yet-fellow citizens that he studied was one of inequality, of imbalance of power. Corporate sponsorship of empirical research was a rarity, given the largely *laissez-faire* theory of the state and the absence of large philanthropic foundations interested in sponsoring research. Relations between scientists and sponsors were simplified by the widespread acceptance of the positivist notion that the facts were there anyway and that it was a matter of expediency to choose best how to discover them. Gatekeepers existed in the form of factory managers, colonial administrators and keepers of official and unofficial archives, but they seem not to have caused difficulties. Scientists were treated as members of a privileged elite, to whom access could safely be granted in the name of science.

Sociology and Social Anthropology Between the Wars

At our second chosen point of historical development, roughly the period between the two world wars, a somewhat different pattern of social inquiry appears. By this time empirical research in the social sciences had been institutionalized. The anthropologist was a recognized and sometimes derided figure in the colonial world, while in the industrialized parts of the world, above all in the United States, sociologists and other social scientists were actively engaged in regular inquiries on a wide range of topics. In British Africa, and to a lesser extent elsewhere in the tropics, this period was the heyday of the doctrine of Indirect Rule, in which ethnographic information had a key part. Disguises began to be used to protect the identity of informants and of the localities in which they lived, as for exmple with the Lynds' well-known study of Muncie in the United States, disguised as 'Middletown' (Lynd & Lynd, 1929). Nevertheless, apart from the use of pseudonyms, little attention was paid to the process of data collection and analysis as affecting the interests of the citizens being studied. Indeed it was at this stage that studies were being made at the General Electric plant outside Chicago (Roethlisberger & Dickson, 1939), that led to the discovery of the Hawthorne effect.

Social scientists made the discovery that, in certain industrial contexts, the factor that led to the greatest increase in productivity was not better lighting, re-arranged seating, rescheduled rest periods or changes in style of supervision but simply the fact of being studied by a team of sympathetic social scientists (Dickson & Roethlisberger, 1966 : 19-36). In retrospect this discovery may seem trite, as is inevitable with most sociological discoveries, for we may reasonably expect human beings to be fairly well informed about how their own social institutions work. What is surprising is that this particular discovery came as a surprise. In fact it was the first significant nail in the coffin of the natural science paradigm as used in social science, for it drew attention to the fact that the interaction between scientist and citizen is two-way, and that the process of inquiry itself has consequences for both the parties. Yet a full appreciation of this discovery was not reached at this period. The identity of the workers investigated in the Hawthorne study was disguised, and all information about their life outside the factory gates was omitted from the published report in order to conceal their identity more effectively. But the book contains no mention of participation by the workers studied in the preparation of the report, nor do I know of any account of the local impact of its publication.

As for anthropologists, they found themselves at this period in an increasingly equivocal position, at least in British colonies. The doctrine of Indirect Rule entailed a thorough analysis of native institutions, so that these could be constructively adapted to the changed conditions of latter-day colonialism. Anthropologists were in some sense experts hired to supply specialist information for the benefit of local administrators, but for most of them the local administration was a gatekeeper rather than a sponsor. Whatever the ultimate source of his funds might be, the pluralist structure of the metropolitan country enabled the field anthropologist to appear under the aegis of an autonomous sponsor, seeking permission from the colonial government to carry out his research by being granted access to native reserves and, perhaps, also to government files. A few colonial governments employed anthropologists or sociologists as regular public servants but no tribe was in a position to hire its own social scientist, even on a temporary basis.

In parenthesis it is interesting to note that one of the very few anthropologists so far to become a head of state is an African who wrote a monograph on his own tribe, the Gikuyu. But the Gikuyu of Kenya did not hire Jomo Kenyatta (1938) as an anthropologist to come and study them; he wrote out of his own experience.

Dependent on the goodwill of government acting as gatekeeper if not as sponsor, but equally dependent on the goodwill of the people they had come to study, anthropologists frequently found themselves subject to crossfire from which they could not easily escape by sitting on the fence. To mix metaphors further, we may say that they tended to bury their heads in the sand. As Gouldner puts it

> Anthropologists ignored problems of imperialism and of the conditions underlying native struggles for national independence. That they shied away from these problems was not due to the absence of opportunity. It was rather that this anthropology operated within the context of an imperialism and colonialism that were under increasing pressure.

He goes on to say that while anthropological research was able to facilitate the administration of tribal peoples, the anthropologist was forced to lead a double life. 'If anthropologists played a role for English colonialism, they also viewed themselves as the paternalistic protectors of indigenous tribal institutions and culture.' Having abandoned the evolutionism that characterized anthropology before 1920, the functional anthropologists of the inter-war years did not take it for granted that native societies were destined to become industrialized or independent. Thus 'While some functional anthropologists conceived it their societal duty to educate colonial administrators, none thought it [his] duty to tutor native revolutionaries' (Gouldner, 1970 : 130-2).

Gouldner is generalizing about anthropologists everywhere during the period when functionalism was dominant, from say 1930 to 1960. Obviously there are many cases that do not tally with his characterization. In particular, his comments would have to be substantially modified before they could be applied to India (cf. Beteille, 1974 : 29). Nevertheless I think he does go some way to explain the tendency of anthropologists during this period to be more sensitive to the interests of the people they studied when these interests were derived from traditional codes of values, as for example in maintaining the secrecy of ritual and symbols, and less responsive towards newly-found native interests such as a greater opportunity to grow cash crops, to earn higher wages and to achieve radical political change. There were, of course, exceptions to this tendency, notably in the work of Godfrey Wilson (1941-2; cf. Brown, 1973).

The inter-war period, from about 1920 to 1940, was thus characterized by the beginnings of an appreciation among social scientists that the natural science paradigm, with its one-way channel between the scientist and the object he studies, was not appropriate to the social sciences or that, so far as sociology and social anthropology are concerned, its application is limited to a few special contexts. On the other hand, there was as yet only a limited appreciation of the methodological implications of adopting an alternative paradigm characterized by the existence of feedback between scientist and citizens, and consequently only a slight awareness of the ethical implications of the new model.

Social Inquiry in Advanced Industrial Society

The process of social inquiry has been altered greatly by the changes that have taken place in the wider society during the last thirty years. Some of the changes, and their effects on social investigation, will have been apparent in the examples presented in my second lecture, for almost all my data were drawn from the present period. The major change affecting social iniquity is, in my view, the incorporation of social science as an integral part of the culture of the advanced industrial societies, and of many societies that at present are largely unindustrialized. The use of the methods of inquiry of social science and the application of its findings have become an essential aspect of the machinery of government. Social science constitutes a large part of all major universities except for the most old-fashioned, and propositions derived from the professional literature of social science appear in transformed guise in newspapers and popular weekly magazines. Technical terms like 'status symbol' and 'conspicuous consumption' have become part of popular speech. The market research investigator, with her clipboard and list of questions about preference for washing powders, no longer has to explain to suburban housewives what she is doing; they know already. In this cultural milieu, relations between social scientists and sponsors, gatekeepers and citizens are no longer the same, but the changes that have occurred since the inter-war period have not all been in the same direction.

Consider first the sponsors. Governments have become more important as sponsors for social scientists and at the same time have greatly increased the extent to which they intervene in the economy and in the social lives of citizens. Indeed the growth of the importance of governments *vis-a-vis* social science research is merely a minor consequence of their growth in other fields. As the range of governmental activity has increased, so has the power of government, so that governments not only provide more of the funds for social research but are in a better position to determine how and when the research shall be done, and are more inclined to exercise their power in this direction. In the nineteenth century, as we have seen, proto-social-scientists collected facts in the hope that governments might use them, while in the inter-war years governments themselves collected a great deal of information as an aid to the formulation and implementation of public policy. This latter mode of using social science continues at the present time and probably accounts for the greater part of all governmental activity as a social science sponsor. But since the end of the Second World War, and I think only since then, a new style of sponsorship has appeared that raises major questions of ethics. It is only recently that governments have begun to envisage seriously the possibility of social engineering, the conscious and deliberate alteration of the parameters of social life so as to bring about some socially desired and scientifically predicted end.

The innocuous beginnings of this new procedure can be seen, for example, in relation to that other recently recognized social process or magic symbol, 'development'. As a natural extension of decades of scientifically conducted field trials in agriculture, and boosted somewhat by the wartime success of operational research, innumerable experiments and action programmes were carried out throughout the tropical world in the '40s and '50s with the twin objects of discovering the most effective conditions for encouraging peasants to grow more crops, or dig more contour ridges, or form thriving cooperative societies, and then of reproducing these same optimum conditions over a wide area. Applied anthropology emerged as an idea during the period of Indirect Rule but it came really to life only in the post-war period of Development. There are analogues of this kind of social engineering in metropolitan countries, particularly in the fields of industrial psychology (Baritz, 1960) and town planning, but the clearest examples are, I think, to be found in the colonial setting for it is there, as we have seen, that we find the closest approach to the natural science paradigm, with minimal feedback from the citizens who are being engineered into a better world.

Like Calvin Coolidge's parson, who was against sin, so are most of us against hunger. Hence any possible clash of interests arising out of a government-sponsored attempt at social engineering to produce more food is likely to remain latent, at least initially. But some attempts at social engineering have been less ostensibly beneficial to mankind. The most famous, or notorious, attempt in recent times is Project Camelot.

Knowledge as Power

Project Camelot came to public notice in June 1965 when, amid a great deal of publicity and controversy, it was abruptly cancelled. It was intended to have been a very large project, with funds of upwards of six million dollars provided by the Office of the Chief of Research and Development of the United States Department of the Army. It was described as a basic social science research project, concerned with the preconditions of internal conflict and with the effects of action taken by local governments in easing, exacerbating or resolving these preconditions. The project was based on the assumption that increased knowledge of this problem would enable the United States Army to cope more effectively with internal revolutions in other nations. Empirical research in various countries in Latin America was called for, and eventually elsewhere in the world as well. The project was organized by a unit nominally part of the American University, Washington, D.C., with the distinctly non-academic name of SORO, Special Operations Research Office (Horowitz, 1967b : 47-67).

Project Camelot raises two sets of ethical questions: those relating to the way the project started and those that arise from the way the project came to an abrupt and premature end. The project was cancelled by Robert McNamara, as Secretary of Defence, in response to pressure from the State Department and from the American Ambassador to Chile, who had not known that discussions about the project had been going on in Chile until the project came under attack from Left-wing Chilean politicians. In the ensuing uproar and debate a good deal of information about the project became public knowledge.

The research design of the project was based on the twin assumptions that revolutions are always bad and that the job of the American Army is to prevent them from succeeding, or preferably to prevent them from occurring, anywhere in the world. It seems that in the United States the sponsorship and aims of the project were not kept secret but in Chile, for one reason or another, the Army's link with the project was not mentioned when it was first discussed with leading academics. A Norwegian sociologist who had been invited to join the project but who had refused to do so on political and ethical grounds brought it to the attention of Chilean intellectuals. The Ambassador was kept in ignorance because of a long-standing rivalry between the American Departments of State and Defence about who should sponsor research of this kind in foreign countries. It is not clear whether the attempt to conceal the sponsorship, or the very existence, of the project formed an essential part of the research design or whether it arose by accident and bad management. In either case the project was based on the premises that in the name of scientific understanding the United States Army has a right to investigate how to abort revolutions in countries like Chile. But science has no respect for national sovereignties, and if we acknowledge the existence of this right, it follows that countries like Chile also have a right to investigate how to abort revolutions in the United States. It is most unlikely that the American Department of the Army would have conceded this right to Chile, and quite unthinkable that it would have conceded to Chile the second right it claimed for itself, the right to use the knowledge gained by the investigation to practical effect, to inhibit revolutions in a foreign country.

When the aims of the project became known to Chileans, their objections, coupled with those of the American Ambassador, were strong enough to lead McNamara to cancel the project. Can we argue that this shows that the inquiry could have been made only in secret, and that it was analogous to those psychological experiments where deception is an essential part of the research design? I think not. Chilean reactions to the disclosure of the aims and sponsorship of the project endangered the success of State Department policies, and the project was therefore cancelled in the hope that the danger would be removed, not because the disclosure invalidated the investigation. Had the investigators not been American, or not been sponsored by the Army, it might have been possible to carry out the investigatory aspects of the project successfully. Indeed, one American commentator on the incident suggested that the inquiry might better have been organized by the United Nations (Bernard, 1965 ; cf. Sjoberg, 1967a : 145).

There is another reason why Project Camelot was not like a psychological experiment involving deception. The aim of experimental work in social psychology is to arrive at propositions about relations between psychologically significant attributes, not about the characteristics of the individuals who happen to participate in the experiments. By and large, this aim is achieved. Field sciences like sociology, social anthropology and political science have similar aims, but so far have been less successful in achieving them. What emerges from the typical field inquiry in these disciplines is a set of statements about the aggregated or even non-aggregated attributes of particular entities—tribes, or nation-states or sample populations—with fairly tentative indications about how these findings might generate abstract propositions about relations between social variables which would be eternally and ubiquitously true. In Project Camelot, the stated aim was to discover general laws about the preconditions for revolution, but it seems that all of value that was likely to emerge, had the Project not been cancelled, would have been information about what social forces in each of the countries investigated tended to promote or inhibit revolutionary trends. As Horowitz says of the project:

> . . . . it was difficult to determine whether it was to be a study of comparative social structures, a set of case studies of single nations 'in depth', or a study of social structure with particular emphasis on the military. In addition, there was a lack of treatment of what indicators were to be used, and whether a given social system in Nation A could be stable in Nation B. [Horowitz, 1965 : 46; cf. Sjoberg, 1967a : 148].

In several social sciences it is inevitable, at their present stage of development, that they should be largely concerned with the attributes of individuals—whether these are persons or communities or nations—rather than with systematic relations between abstracted variables. The difficulty of paying proper attention to considerations of privacy and confidentiality is thereby increased.

Another feature of Project Camelot I find even more objectionable. All the social scientists engaged in planning the project appear to have accepted without question the legitimacy of the American army's claim to investigate the preconditions of revolution and then to use this knowledge to prevent them from occuring. Although the director of the project selected a notably liberal-minded team of scientists to assist him, the project was planned on the assumption that a stable society is the normal, as well as the desired, state of affairs. 'The breakdown of social order' is spoken of accusatively, says Horowitz, who remarks that, 'It never seemed to occur to its personnel to inquire into the desirability for successful revolutions . . . in nearly every page of the various working papers, there are assertions which clearly derive from American military policy objectives rather than scientific method' (Horowitz, 1965 : 46-7). I agree with Sjoberg (1967a : 157) when he explains this by the failure of the social scientists in Project Camelot to preserve their autonomy. They had over-identified themselves with their sponsors, partly through failure in seeing that by acting as if they were simply employees of the army they were betraying the disinterested and impartial values of the academic world under whose banner they were claiming to operate and partly because, as Sjoberg says, 'American social scientists (including sociologists) have been socialized, both as citizens and scholars, to an almost unquestioning acceptance of the authority and power wielded by their own nation-state and consequently the administrative controls of the national government'. Sjoberg comments that 'Nationalism is perhaps the most pervasive, yet the least explored, of the influences that shape the research carried out by American social scientists in other nations'. As a third reason he notes that professional organizations, particularly those of social scientists whose claims to higher social prestige are still not fully endorsed, encourage their members to maintain a position of respectability in the eyes of the broader society by forging links with the major institutional systems of that society.

Sjoberg was writing of American social scientists in 1967. The ensuing eight years have perhaps brought a keener critical and anti-Establishment spirit into the academic scene, yet what he has to say remains generally true, and his comments must apply equally accurately to many countries besides the United States. I well remember the response of one of my own teachers, Evans-Pritchard, when he heard about a cooperative effort by administrators and anthropologists in Africa in which I had been involved as a very junior scientist. The effort was, I still think, entirely benign and justified, and was beneficial to the citizens we studied. Nevertheless I could see the force of Evans-Pritchard's comment : 'He who sups with the administration needs a long spoon.' I hope that by analysing the process of social inquiry, and by realizing that relations between scientists and their sponsors and gatekeepers require as much careful definition as do relations between scientists and citizens, we may be able to avoid some of the mistakes made in Project Camelot.

I cannot discuss all the ethical and political issues arising out of the cancellation of the project but I will mention one aspect of the cancellation that bears on my main line of argument. Two months after McNamara's decision President Johnson issued a memorandum prohibiting the use of federal funds for the support of foreign area research except with the approval of the Secretary of State (Horowitz, 1965 : 5). Here we have an unequivocal statement of the view that social research must be subordinate to foreign policy. The order may not have been intended to restrict overseas research to those projects which, it was thought, would positively assist American foreign policy, but it was certainly aimed at eliminating projects that endangered its success. The order embodies the premise that knowledge, including the knowledge gained from the inquiries of social scientists, is potentially or actually a source of power. The same view was assumed by the American army in sponsoring the project, and was also held by those Chileans who protested at the envisaged use of American power against them. In one sense, of course, all applied science represents the use of scientific knowledge as a source of power to change the world, so that even the members of the Statistical Society of London, when collecting statistics on drunkenness and prostitution in the early nineteenth century, subscribed to the same premises. But there is a difference of degree. Private gentlemen collecting useful statistics in the hope that government might be moved by them or, at the next stage, government anthropologists collecting information on tribal marriage customs in the 1930s, so that the law could be properly codified; these reflect a much milder appreciation of knowledge as power than we find in Project Camelot. The instrumental perception of knowledge was taken a large step forward when, in the Project, an army, rather than a civilian branch of government, decided to spend six million dollars not on military hardware but on social science research. Many social scientists would hesitate to put so high a monetary or practical value on their usually tentative research findings, but the American army must have thought otherwise.

The perception of knowledge derived from social science as power may have been taken a stage further a few years later by, not surprisingly, the CIA. According to some reports, in its operations in Indo-China the CIA selected targets for its bombers partly on the basis of ethnographic information collected by anthropologists and other social scientists working in the region. In this episode which, like Project Camelot, became the object of intense professional controversy but where the facts of the case are even harder to establish, we have been shown in the bluntest possible form that field scientists must recognize that they do not carry on their inquiries in an academic ivory tower. They have to gather their data and disseminate their findings in a world in which the interests of citizens, sponsors, gatekeepers and others, as well as of themselves, are all likely to differ fundamentally. I agree with Silvert, another commentator on Project Camelot, when he says that 'I do not believe that our present state of ethical disarray has created a Frankenstein's monster rapidly conducing us to the socially engineered society. It is this possibility which frightened some Chileans inordinately' (Silvert, 1966 : 151 ; cf. Sjoberg, 1967a : 147; Horowitz, 1967b : 92). The nightmare or utopia of an engineered society may depend on the discovery of generalizations and law-like propositions that, for better or worse, still elude our most earnest efforts, as social scientists. Nevertheless, our failure to discover the laws of social change does not, alas, hindeı us from using data on political alliances in particular tribal villages for the selection of bombing targets.

The growth of the notion of knowledge as power has been brought about by a shift in the balance of power, and only to a minor extent by the growth of our scientific understanding of society. Governments in industrialized societies, both capitalist and communist, have become more powerful and their pluralist characteristics have been eroded. The social scientist is no longer the elite gentleman of private means but is a propertyless professional dependent on support from a sponsor. If a private foundation or independent-minded university can support him, he may be able to negotiate terms so that he can fulfil his obligations to the citizens he studies as well as to his sponsor. The less pluralist the society he works in, the harder it is for him to protect the interests of the citizens as well as to defend his own interests. Writing in 1967 Sjoberg (1967a : 155) comments hopefully:

> Of considerable theoretical significance also is the emerging situation in the Soviet Union. Considerable evidence indicates that Soviet researchers are struggling to legitimize and institutionalize their activities. This is, however, proving difficult because the administrative control functions of the Party (and the State) are given clear priority. In fact, except for certain

> present-day intellectuals, Marxist theoreticians in the U.S.S.R have denied the existence of a 'private sector' for either persons or organizations apart from the Party or State.

Whether Sjoberg's hopes have been fulfilled is doubtful. There is however no doubt of the importance of maintaining a proper separation of function, and a very careful check on the flow of information, between scientist and sponsor, whoever the latter may be, if the interests of citizens are to be respected. This is not simply a matter of ethics, but also of tactics. The procedures of inquiry followed in social science are based on the assumption that citizens are free to answer questions and offer information as they please and that, under favourable conditions, they will speak sincerely. An interview with a social scientist is not an interrogation by the police. Writing of social inquiry in Brazil after the military coup, Horowitz (1967a : 220) says, 'When the formal, procedural aspects of democracy are erased by political fiat, then attitude questionnaires become empty, devoid of sociological content. . . . It is a curious but real fact that many sociological techniques depend upon mass democracy for their validity.' I would not restrict the validity of the social survey and other techniques as narrowly as Horowitz does, for there are, for instance, many tribal communities where the formal, procedural aspects of democracy have never been known but where the citizens are only too ready to express their attitudes sincerely and volubly. Yet clearly unless citizens feel they have the right to comment freely on their social environment, the scientist cannot attach much weight to what they tell him.

This commitment to pluralism on technical grounds is reinforced by the social scientist's broader commitment to seek knowledge wherever it may be found. As Srinivas (1966 : 163) puts it, 'The sociologist's commitment to democratic processes is fundamental . . . for unfettered social inquiry cannot exist and flourish in totalitarian systems'. He goes on to comment: 'This is particularly true in regard to a sociologist studying his own society.'

Knowledge as Property

Although concentration of power may be seen as a threat to pluralist democracy, the growth in the power of governments in industrialized societies since 1945 has to some extent been counterbalanced by two parallel growths which strengthen pluralism. On the one hand the nations of the Third World that have emerged from colonial status have been able to gather their strength, while on the other the citizens, particularly in Western industrialized countries but doubtless in some other countries as well, have become more conscious of their collective power in relation to governments and more able to organize themselves to exercise this power.

We may say that nowadays, whereas sponsors in the advanced industrial societies tend to treat the findings of social science as a source of power, gatekeepers in Third World countries, and some social scientists as well, seem to regard both the findings of social science, and the data on which these findings are based, as a form of property. Much the same attitude is taken by groups of citizens in industrialized countries. In the first lecture I noted that in some instances Blacks in the United States refuse to complete questionnaires or to give interviews when the field social scientist is White. This should not surprise us in a country where, for hundreds of years, Whites have similarly refused to answer questions or enter into discussions when the social scientist has been Black. Yet this new attitude taken by Blacks is not simply a reflection of a shift in the balance of power, though clearly that is part of the explanation. What is new is the extension of the notion of privacy to embrace not only information about oneself but also any scientific, or indeed non-scientific, conclusions that might be drawn from aggregating this information with similar information about other individuals. This extension is partly due to adopting the notion that knowledge is power, but it has other causes as well. For there has been a shift in attitudes away from positivism. I am not, of course, suggesting that citizens at large think in terms of this notion but the shift in their attitudes can best be explained by reference to it. Instead of believing that true facts about social phenomena exist objectively and can be discovered by anyone who uses appropriate objective techniques, more people are now inclined to take the view that individuals and groups construct their own versions of reality, their own folk ontology, and see the world always through spectacles of local or individual manufacture. More importantly, although they stress the need for inter-subjectivity for understanding how the other person sees things, at the same time they deny that this can be achieved by outsiders. A man can never understand the woman's point of view, a White can never comprehend what it is like to be Black, an atheist cannot realize what it means to have faith in a god. There is some truth in these views and they are not new. What is new is the insistence that because a White cannot completely comprehend being Black, therefore his partial understanding is worthless; and the same is true of any other attempt to bridge the gulf between one group and another.

In part, then, the revolt of the citizens, if we may call it that, is simply an insistence that they are citizens, that they have rights and that if social scientists, or agents of the government, or any other busybody wants information, they cannot get it simply on demand; there must be some negotiation. Knowledge is seen as property, but as property for which there is an open market. In this sense the revolt of the citizens is similar to the revolt of the consumers which has led to the formation of consumers' associations that attempt, in effect, to negotiate with the producers of commodities and services on a basis of equality. But at the same time as more and more citizens insist on 'no transaction without negotiation', some citizens now deny that there is any basis for negotiation at all, except within their own group. Hence the rise of courses in Black studies, taught by Blacks and designed only for Blacks. In their wake are courses on women, taught by women and intended mainly or exclusively for women. Thus the notion of a unified and universal social science begins to disappear, to be replaced by Black sociology, White sociology, the sociology of women, the sociology of men, and so on, each with its own impenetrable mystique. Under these circumstances, knowledge is not merely property; it is unalienable private property, or property with a very restricted market.

I welcome the citizens' insistence on negotiation but regret that some citizens are not prepared to negotiate at all with me unless I happen to belong to their group, as they define it. It may be that Black studies in the United States are already on the wane, but it seems as though for some time still to come there will be tension within the women's movement between, on the one hand, the tendency to extend to the field of knowledge that exclusiveness which may well be necessary in the field of organization to achieve an effective common purpose, and on the other the desire to utilize such power as is available from the achievements of a universal social science.

I have used women and Blacks to illustrate my thesis of citizens in revolt but the questions they raise may be applied with only slight modification to scientists in countries that have not yet become industrialized and where social science is seen as an importation from the West. With the change from colonial to independent status there has been a change in the balance of power. Poverty prevents Third World governments from playing much of a role as sponsors, at least on the scale of Project Camelot, and private sponsors in these countries are few and far between. Newly independent governments have however soon realized their power as gatekeepers and in many cases have used it freely. Thus, for example, before allowing foreigners to undertake social research in their territories various governments have insisted that the topics selected for study shall be relevant to the national purpose, as defined by them (cf. Dube, 1973 : 21). Some have required foreign field scientists to train local students as research assistants or have insisted that copies of all publications or dissertations, or even field notes, shall be deposited in the country concerned, so that what benefits there may be from the research may accrue at once to the locality and not merely to the world of learning. Students in Third World countries have sometimes been just as demanding as their governments. For example, in the British Solomon Islands Protectorate, in the south Pacific, a recent student writer demands that a certain anthropologist should forego the fantastic income he will gain through publishing the results of his researches and should instead use the money to finance scholarships for children in the group he studied (Waleurifo, 1973 : 11). In Papua New Guinea other students undergoing training in sociological fieldwork have protested against, as they see it, being used as cheap labour to enable members of the teaching staff to gain higher academic qualifications (Powell, 1974 : 222).

The procedures adopted by Third World governments, extremely tiresome as they may sometimes seem to be, are, as I hope I have shown, essentially the same as those followed by other gatekeepers and sponsors in metropolitan countries. Because governments, even in the Third World, are relatively powerful, field research carried out under these conditions imposes a particularly heavy responsibility on the scientist if he is to preserve his own autonomy and protect the interests of the citizens. Likewise the attitudes of students in Third World countries do not differ much from the attitudes of their counterparts in the West. Even the demand for scholarships is an echo of the tactic adopted by Keiser, an anthropologist who studied a Black gang called the Vice Lords in Chicago.

Describing his work, he says 'I explained that I wanted to write a book about the Vice Lords and offered to share my royalties with the group' (Keiser, 1970: 227).

There are also parallels between the attitudes of Blacks and liberated women with those adopted by some social scientists in Third World countries. There is the same recognition of the need to increase the cohesion and sense of identity of the group, to establish a self-conscious and intellectually autonomous profession, and to limit its dependence on foreigners (Uberoi, 1968). Similarly there is a secondary tendency to deny the possibility of inter-subjectivity and shared cognitive assumptions between groups, and to argue that so-called universal social science is merely Western social science; a newly independent country must not only prove its independence by establishing its own profession of social science but must also develop its own set of analytical concepts and its intuitive insights or testable propositions (Madan, 1972: 289, 304). Some of the writers who have sometimes given the impression of holding this view have indicated that in fact they still adhere to the notion of a universal social science (Madan, 1967) but I think that it is nevertheless a view that has to be taken seriously and rebutted explicitly.

For just as I find this second tendency understandable but undesirable among women and Blacks, I find it understandable but still undesirable in newly independent countries and, for that matter, in countries that have long been independent as well. No-one argues in favour of developing a Black physics or a women's geology or a Patagonian chemistry, for these disciplines belong to the natural sciences, where universality is accepted and validated. We can still remember the absurdity of a distinctively Soviet genetics; but in fact Lysenko claimed that his theories operated universally and not merely within the boundaries of the Soviet Union. For the same reason we cannot appeal to the contrast between Marxist and bourgeois sociology, which some protagonists see as irreconcilably distinct, for each claims to be universal and to encompass the other. I endorse Uberoi's position when, speaking of social scientists in India, he says, 'For us the important considerations should be to define our relevant problems and pursue their solutions, not worrying about the sources of ideas; that task can be left to be performed by our intellectual biographers' (Abbi & Saberwal, 1969 : 192)

Particularist social sciences are feasible only if we assume that the social sciences are not sciences at all. By science I mean a process whereby models of reality embodying potentially falsifiable hypotheses are continually matched against objective empirical evidence and are tentatively retained only until they can be replaced by better approximations to reality. To rehearse the arguments for and against the view that, in this sense, the social sciences are indeed part of science I would need another set of lectures. If the social sciences are truly only humanities dolled up in the jargon of real science, then the way is open to construct, among other things, a distinctively Indian sociology, as several Indian scholars have advocated. Against this view, I can, in this context, merely assert that I agree with Dumont (1966 : 23) when he says that 'A Hindu sociology is a contradiction in terms'. In these lectures I have taken this major issue for granted (cf. Bandopadhyay, 1971) and have tried to merely demonstrate that the differences between the natural and social sciences do not in themselves compromise the scientific status of social science, in the sense that I have indicated. At the same time I have tried to show why and in what ways these differences make the task of the social sciences more difficult. It is the hardness of the intellectual tasks they tackle and the softness of the data they have to analyse that explain why so far their achievements cannot match those of the natural sciences.

The hardness of social science springs in part from the feedback that takes place between the scientist and the citizens he studies, and it is through this feedback process, the two-way interaction between the scientist and his sponsors as well as with citizens and gatekeepers, that ethical problems arise in the course of social inquiry. In the second lecture I presented a number of diverse ethical points that have arisen in cases of fieldwork and which were solved well or poorly or were ignored. In this third lecture I have provided a very rough sketch of trends in the pattern of relations between the four components of our model of the process of social inquiry. Not all the cases cited conform to these trends and obviously the trends operate at different rates in various regional and topical contexts. Nevertheless I hope that, rather than relying on the application of a formal timeless code of ethics or of tackling each new instance from first principles, a realization of the broad picture of historical transition may help towards the satisfactory resolution of specific ethical problems.

References

ABBI, Behari Lal & SABERWAL, Satish (eds.) 1969 — 'Urgent Research in Social Anthropology: proceedings of a conference', *Transactions, vol.* 10, Indian Institute of Advanced Study, Simla.

ABRAMS, Philip 1968 — *The Origins of British Sociology : 1834-1914, an essay with selected papers*, University of Chicago Press, Chicago.

ASCH, Solomon Elliott 1956 — 'Studies of Independence and Submission to Group Pressure : I, A minority of one against a unanimous majority, *Psychological Monographs : General and Applied*, 70 (9), no. 416.

BANDHOPADHYAY, Pradeep 1971 — 'One Sociology or Many : some issues in radical sociology', *Sociological Review*, n.s. 19, pp. 5-29.

BARITZ, Loren 1960 — *The Servants of Power : a history of the use of social science in American industry*, Wesleyan University Press, Middletown, Conn.

BATESON, Gregory 1958 — *Naven : a survey of the problems suggested by a composite picture of the culture of a New Guinea tribe drawn from three points of view,* 2nd ed., Stanford University Press, Stanford.

BECKER, Howard & BARNES, Harry Elmer 1961 — *Social Thought from Lore to Science*, 3rd ed., vol., 1 Dover, New York.

BERNARD, Jessie 1965 — Letter to the editor, *American Sociologist,* 1, pp. 24-5.

BERREMAN, Gerald Duane 1972 — *Hindus of the Himalayas : ethnography and change,* 2nd ed., University of California Press, Berkeley.

BETEILLE, Andre
1974 — *Six Essays in Comparative Sociology*, Oxford University Press, Delhi.
1975 — 'The Tribulations of Fieldwork', in Andre Beteille & T.N., Madan (eds.), *Encounter and Experience.*

BETEILLE, Andre & MADAN Triloki Nath 1975 — *Encounter and Experience : personal accounts of fieldwork*, Vikas Publishing House, Delhi.

BRADNEY, Pamela 1957 — 'The Joking Relationship in Industry', *Human Relations*, 10, pp. 179-87.

BROEDER, Dale W.
1959 — 'The University of Chicago Jury Project', *Nebraska Law Review*, 38, pp. 744-60.
1960 — 'Silence and Perjury before Police Officers : an examination of the criminal law risks, *Nebraska*

Law Review, 40, pp. 63-103.

BROWN, Paula 1954 — 'Bureaucracy in a Government Laboratory', *Social Forces*, 32, pp. 259-68.

BROWN, Richard 1973 — 'Anthropology and Colonial Rule: the case of Godfrey Wilson and the Rhodes-Livingstone Institute, Northern Rhodesia, *in* Talal Asad (ed.), *Anthropology and the Colonial Encounter*, Ithaca Press, London, pp. 173-97.

BRYMER, Richard Aubrey & FARRIS, Buford 1967 — 'Ethical and Political Dilemmas in the Investigation of Deviance: a study of juvenile delinquency', *in* Gideon Sjoberg (ed)., *Ethics, Politics, and Social Research*, pp. 297-318.

CAMBRIDGE ANTHROPOLOGICAL EXPEDITION TO TORRES STRAITS 1901-35 — *Reports*, Cambridge University Press, Cambridge, 6 vols.

CAUDILL, William 1958 — *The Psychiatric Hospital as a Small Society*, Harvard University Press, Cambridge, Mass.

CAUDILL, William, REDLICH, Fredrick Carl, GILMORE, Helen R. & BRODY, Eugene B. 1952 — 'Social Structure and Interaction Processes on a Psychiatric Ward', *American Journal of Orthopsychiatry*, 22, pp. 314-34.

DANIELS, Arlene Kaplan 1967 — 'The Low-Caste Stranger in Social Research', *in* Gideon Sjoberg (ed.), *Ethics, Politics, and Social Research*, pp. 267-96.

DE VOS, George, & VOGEL, Ezra Feivel 1973 — 'Achievement, Culture and Personality: the case of William Caudill', *Journal of Nervous and Mental Disease*, 157, pp. 232-6.

DICKSON, William John & ROETHLISBERGER, Fritz Jules 1966 — *Counseling in an Organization : a sequel to the Hawthorne researches*, Harvard University (Graduate School of Business Administration, Division of Research), Boston.

DUBE, Shyama Charan 1973 — *Social Sciences in Changing Society : D.N. Majumdar Lectures* 1972, Ethnographic and Folk Culture Society of U.P., Lucknow.

DUMONT, Louis 1966 — 'A Fundamental Problem in the Sociology of Caste', *Contributions to Indian Sociology*, 9, pp. 17-32.

GOFFMAN, Erving 1969 — *The Presentation of Self in Everyday Life*, Allen Lane, the Penguin Press, London.

GOULDNER, Alvin Ward 1970 — *The Coming Crisis of Western Sociology*, Basic Books, New York.

HADDON, Alfred Cort — 'General Ethnography', *in Reports of the Cam-*

1935 *bridge Anthropological Expedition to Torres Straits*, vol. 1, Cambridge University Press, Cambridge.

1901 *Head-Hunters—Black, White, and Brown*, Methuen, London.

HART, Charles William Merton 1970 'Fieldwork Among the Tiwi, 1928-1929', *in* George Dearborn Spindler (ed.), *Being An Anthropologist*, pp. 142-63.

HOLMBERG, Allan Richard 1969 'Nomads of the Long Bow : the Siriono of eastern Bolivia', *American Museum Science Books B. 20*, Natural History Press, Garden City, N.Y .

HOROWITZ, Irving Louis 1965 'The Life and Death of Project Camelot', *Transactions* 3(1), 3-7, 44-7.

1967a 'The Natural History of Revolution in Brazil : a biography of a book', *in* Gideon Sjoberg (ed.), *Ethics, Politics, and Social Research*, pp. 198-224.

1967b (ed.) *The Rise and Fall of Project Camelot : studies in the relationship between social science and practical politics*, M.I.T. Press, Cambridge, Mass.

JAQUES, Elliott 1951 *The Changing Culture of a Factory*, Tavistock, London.

KAY, James Phillips 1838 'On the establishment of county or district schools, for the training of the pauper children maintained in union workhouses', *Journal of the Statistical Society of London*, 1, pp. 14-27.

KEISER, R. Lincoln 1970 'Fieldwork among the Vice Lords of Chicago', *in* George Dearborn Spindler (ed.), *Being an Anthropologist*, pp. 220-37.

KENYATTA, Jomo 1938 *Facing Mount Kenya: the tribal life of the Gikuyu*, Secker & Warburg, London.

LASZLO, Ervin & WILBUR, James Benjamin (eds.) 1970 *Human Values and Natural Science : proceedings of the third conference on value inquiry*, *Current topics of contemporary thought*, vol. 4,Gorden & Breach, New York.

LEE, Dorothy 1948 'Are Basic Needs Ultimate?' *Journal of Abnormal and Social Psychology*, 43, pp. 391-5.

LYND, Robert Staughton, & LYND, Helen Merrell 1929 *Middletown : a study in contemporary American culture*, Harcourt Brace, New York.

MADAN, Triloki Nath 1965 *Family and Kinship : a study of the Pandits of rural Kashmir*, Asia Publishing House, Bombay.

1967 'For a Sociology of India : some clarifications', *Contributions to Indian Sociology*, n.s., 1., pp. 90-3.

1972 'Research Methodology : a trend report', *in* Indian Council of Social Science Research, *A Survey of*

Research in Sociology and Social Anthropology, vol. III, Popular Prakashan, Bombay, pp. 282-315

1975 — 'On Living Intimately with Strangers', *in* Andre, Beteille, and T.N. Madan (eds.), *Encounter and Experience*, pp. 131-56

MILGRAM, Stanley
1974 — *Obedience to Authority : an experimental view*, Harper & Row, New York.

O'NEILL, John
1972 — *Sociology as a Skin Trade: essays toward a reflexive sociology*, Harper & Row, New York.

ORLANS, Harold
1967 — 'Ethical Problems in the Relations of Research Sponsors and Investigators', *in* Gideon Sjoberg (ed.), *Ethics, Politics, and Social Research*, pp. 3-24

PANDEY, Triloki Nath
1975 — ' "India man" among American Indians', *in* Andre Beteille and T.N. Madan (eds.), *Encounter and Experience*, pp. 194-213.

PORTES, Alejandro
1975 — 'Trends in International Research Cooperation: the Latin American case', *American Sociologist*, 10, pp. 131-40.

POWELL, John P.
1974 — 'Attitudes of Melanesian Students to Fieldwork and Research in the Social Sciences', *Mankind*, 9, pp. 218-24.

QUIGGIN, Alison Hingston
1942 — *Haddon the Head Hunter : a short sketch of the life of A.C. Haddon*, Cambridge University Press, Cambridge.

RECORD, Jane Cassels
1967 — 'The Research Institute and the Pressure Group', *in* Gideon Sjoberg, (ed.), *Ethics, Politics, and Social Research*, pp. 45-9.

ROETHLISBERGER, Fritz Jules & DICKSON, William John
1939 — *Management and the Worker : an account of a research program conducted by the Western Electric Company, Hawthorne Works, Chicago*, Harvard University Press, Cambridge, Mass.

ROY, Donald
1952 — 'Quota Restriction and Goldbricking in a Piecework Machine Shop', *American Journal of Sociology*, 57, pp. 427-42.

SCOTT, William Richard
1965 — 'Field Methods in the Study of Organizations', *in* James Gardener March (ed.), *Handbook of Organizations*, Rand McNally, Chicago, pp. 261-304.

SHAW, George Bernard
1971 — *Collected Plays with their Prefaces*, vol. III, Bodley Head, London.

SHILS, Edward Albert
1956 — *The Torment of Secrecy : the background and consequences of American security policies*, Free Press, Glencoe, Ill.

SILVERT, Kalman Hirsch 1966 — *The Conflict Society : reaction and revolution in Latin America*, rev. ed., American Universities Field Staff, New York.

SISSONS, Mary 1971 — 'The Psychology of Social Class', *in* Open University, *Understanding Society : a foundation course, Units* 14-18 : *money, wealth and class,* Open University Press, Bletchiey, pp. 111-31.

SJOBERG, Gideon 1967a — 'Project Camelot : selected reactions and personal reflections', *in* Gideon Sjoberg (ed.), *Ethics, Politics, and Social Research*, pp. 141-61.

1967b (ed.) — *Ethics, Politics, and Social Research*, Schenkman, Cambridge, Mass.

SPINDLER, George Dearborn (ed.) 1970 — *Being an Anthropologist : fieldwork in eleven cultures*, Holt, Rinehart & Winston, New York.

SRINIVAS, Mysore Narasimhachar 1966 — *Social Change in Modern India*, University of California Press, Berkeley.

SRINIVAS, Mysore Narasimhachar & PANINI, M.N. 1973 — 'The Development of Sociology and Social Anthropology in India', *Sociological Bulletin*, 22, pp. 179-215.

UBEROI, Jitendra Pal Singh 1968 — 'Science and Swaraj', *Contributions to Indian Sociology*, n.s. 2, pp. 119-23.

UNNITHAN, Thottamon Kantankesavan Narayanan, SINGH, Yogendra, SINGHI, Narendra & DEVA, Indra (eds.) 1967 — *Sociology for India,* Prentice-Hall of India, New Delhi

VAUGHAN, Ted Ray 1967 — 'Governmental Intervention in Social Research: political and ethical dimensions in the Wichita jury recordings', *in* Gideon Sjoberg (ed.), *Ethics, Politics, and Social Research*, pp. 50-77.

WALEURIFO, I 1973 — 'Cultural Exploiters in the Solomons', *Kakamora Reporter*, 34, pp. 8-12.

WARNER, Malcolm & STONE, Michael 1970 — *The Data Bank Society*, Allen & Unwin, London.

WHYTE, William Foote 1941 — 'The Social Role of the Settlement House', *Applied Anthropology*, 1(1), pp. 14-19.

1955 — *Street Corner Society : the social structure of an Italian slum,* 2nd ed., University of Chicago Press, Chicago.

WILSON, Alexander Thomson Macbeth 1951 — 'Introduction', *in* Elliott Jaques, *The Changing Culture of a Factory*, pp. xiii-xvii

WILSON, Godfrey 1941-2 — 'An Essay on the Economics of Detribalization in Northern Rhodesia, 2 pts., *Rhodes-Livingstone Papers* 5 *and* 6, Rhodes-Livingstone Institute, Livingstone.